This Old Tractor

A Treasury of Vintage Tractors
and Family Farm Memories

Michael Dregni, Editor
Foreword by Roger Welsch

With stories, photographs, and artwork from Ralph W. Sanders, Randy Leffingwell, Roger Welsch, Don Macmillan, Robert N. Pripps, C. H. Wendel, Andrew Morland, Bill Vossler, John Hildebrand, Grant Wood, Thomas Hart Benton, Bob Artley, and more.

TOWN
SQUARE
BOOKS
an imprint of Voyageur Press

Edited by Todd R. Berger
Designed by Andrea Rud
Printed in Hong Kong

98   99   00   01   02   5   4   3   2   1

Library of Congress Cataloging-in-Publication Data
This old tractor : a treasury of vintage tractors and family farm memories / Michael Dregni, editor ; with stories and photographs from
    Ralph W. Sanders . . . [et al.].
        p. cm.
    "A Town Square book."
    Includes index.
    ISBN 0-89658-368-6
    1. Farm tractors—United States—History. 2. Farm tractors—United States—Anecdotes. I. Dregni, Michael, 1961– . II. Sanders,
Ralph W., 1933–
    S711.T48 1998
    631.3'72'092273—dc21   97-44770
                                            CIP
A Town Square Book
Published by Voyageur Press, Inc.   Distributed in Europe by Midland Publishing Ltd.
123 North Second Street, P.O. Box 338, Stillwater, MN 55082 U.S.A.   24 The Hollow, Earl Shilton, Leicester LE9 7NA, England
612-430-2210, fax 612-430-2211   Tel: 01455 233747

Educators, fundraisers, premium and gift buyers, publicists, and marketing managers: Looking for creative products and new sales ideas? Voyageur Press books are available at special discounts when purchased in quantities, and special editions can be created to your specifications. For details contact the marketing department at 800-888-9653.

Permissions
    "Goodbye Horses, Hello Farmall" from *Vintage International Harvester Tractors* by Ralph W. Sanders. Copyright © 1997 by Ralph W. Sanders. Reprinted by permission of the author and Voyageur Press.
    "Tractors" from *The Land Remembers* by Ben Logan. Copyright © 1975 by Ben T. Logan. Reprinted by permission of Frances Collin Literary Agent.
    "Subterfuge" from *All My Meadows* by Patricia Penton Leimbach. Copyright © 1977 by Patricia Penton Leimbach. Reprinted by permission of the author.
    "Threshing Day" by Sara De Luca. Copyright © 1998 by Sara De Luca. Reprinted by permission of the author.
    "Mapping The Farm" from *Mapping the Farm: The Chronicle of a Family* by John Hildebrand. Copyright © 1995 by John Hildebrand. Reprinted by permission of Random House, Inc.
    "The Last Threshing" from *Dancing the Cows Home: A Wisconsin Girlhood* by Sara De Luca, published by the Minnesota Historical Society Press. Copyright © 1996 by Sara De Luca. Reprinted by permission of the author and the Minnesota Historical Society Press.
    "Roger's Rules for Collecting Old Iron and Living with Your Wife" by Roger Welsch. Used by permssion of *Successful Farming* magazine. Copyright © Meredith Corporation.
    Cartoons from *Memories of a Former Kid* by Bob Artley. Copyright © 1978 by Bob Artley. Reprinted by permission of the author.
    Cartoons from *Cartoons II: From the Newspaper Series "Memories of a Former Kid"* by Bob Artley. Copyright © 1989 by Bob Artley. Reprinted by permission of the author.

ON THE ENDPAPERS: *Threshing crew from a bygone era: the McGuire Brothers threshing outfit photographed while on break with their steam traction engine near Stillwater, Minnesota, in 1931. (Photograph by John Runk/Minnesota Historical Society collection)*
ON THE FRONTISPIECE: *Sibling tractors: a 1935 Deere Model B, with an Ertl Company model in the foreground. In the center is a Deere Model 60 pedal tractor. Owner: Allen Martin of Ephrata, Pennsylvania. (Photograph by Keith Baum)*
ON THE TITLE PAGES: *Early morning fog rising from farmland in Lancaster County, Pennsylvania. (Photograph by Jerry Irwin).* INSET ON THE TITLE PAGE: *A Little Bull tractor from 1913 pulls a Deere gang plow. The Bull was a twelve-horsepower, three-wheeled tractor made in Minneapolis, Minnesota. (Robert N. Pripps collection)*

Contents

Acknowledgments

I have been fortunate over the years to have worked with many of the writers and photographers whose essays and illustrations are collected in this book. I would like to thank them as well as others who helped make this book come to life: John O. Allen; Bob Artley, whom I remember from my days at the *Worthington Daily Globe*; Keith Baum; Jean Brookins of the Minnesota Historical Society Press; Sara De Luca; Gale C. Frost, superintendent of the Heritage Exhibits, Minnesota State Fair; Ken Giannini of the Minnesota State Fair; Jerry Irwin; Ed Klimuska; Andy Kraushaar; Randy Leffingwell; Patricia Penton Leimbach; Don Macmillan; Vincent Manocchi; Andrew Morland; Max E. Neufeldt; Robert N. Pripps; Gerard W. Rinaldi, publisher of the *9N-2N-8N Newsletter*; Ralph W. Sanders; Claire D. Scheibe, publisher of *Toy Farmer*; Les Stegh, Deere & Company archivist; Bill Vossler; Roger Welsch; and C. H. Wendel.

I would also like to thank Sigrid Arnott, Mark Stanton of Raincoast Books, and Dave Hohman, who had the idea for this book.

Finally, for his help with this project and others, I would like to thank Peter Letourneau, who passed away while I was compiling this book.

Fledgling tractor dealership

ABOVE: *Often taking the place of horse liveries and stables, tractor dealerships sprang up to sell and service the new power farming wares in the 1910s. This Minneapolis Steel & Machinery Company dealership in Saskatoon, Saskatchewan, attracted local farmers who were considering trading in their horses on a new Twin City tractor. (Minnesota Historical Society collection)*

Common sense

FACING PAGE: *The Common Sense gas tractor from the Minneapolis, Minnesota, company of the same name featured a stunning 20/40 V-8 engine. The tractor made its debut in 1915, but even the radical eight-cylinder powerplant could not win it fans; it dropped from the field in 1920. (Minnesota Historical Society collection)*

Foreword

By Roger Welsch

It's a strange thing, this Cult of Old Iron. I know better than to try to explain it to those who have not already been touched by it. Like any love, it's not a matter of logic, or research . . . not a process or condition that can be explained. This passion is simply there—curious to the outsider, irresistible to the insider, mysterious to all.

I have friends whose passions are old Chevys, or Harleys, or flintlock pistols, or windmills. That's all right, I suppose, but I can't say as I see the attraction. I mean, those things are just machines. But restoring, collecting, and loving them doesn't do any harm, so I don't suppose the time and money is entirely wasted.

But, ah, old tractors! Especially Allis Chalmers WCs! Now those are machines worthy of veneration. Objects fit for the love of man and woman alike. Things of beauty . . . the design, the endurance, the history, the tradition.

My own story is instructive and, probably, typical— if in no other way, in that it is utterly peculiar and unique. Some lovers of old tractors have at least the dignity of a superficial explanation for why they do what they do:

"Well, you see, this was my Dad's tractor and I want to keep her running in memory of him. . . ."

"This is the first kind of tractor I had when I started farming, and so it's a matter of tradition for me. . . ."

"My grandpa worked on the assembly line making these machines and so he may have had a part in building this very one. . . ."

"I have wanted a John Deere B since I was just a little kid, so. . . ."

"I bought this place and this old thing was sitting back in a shed. . . ."

"I've always been good at mechanicking, and I saw this one for sale up in town and the price was right. . . ."

Me, I don't have an excuse like that for my passion. Twenty years ago a friend told me he had an old tractor stuck back in some trees near where he once farmed. He said that if I wanted it, I could have it. You know, to clear the lane in the winter, to pull a plow for planting trees (my place is a tree farm), to drag logs around, to haul the garbage trailer to the dump—that kind of thing. Sounded like a great idea to me, even though I had never in my memory so much as touched a tractor, much less sat on one.

In fact, I can almost precisely document every single encounter I had with tractors during the first forty years of my life. There were, after all, only two. When I was a kid, I, uh, "helped" my Uncle Fred put up hay in eastern Wyoming. He had some tractors as I recall. I jumped around on the stacks with Cousin Dick, dug heartily into lunch, washed off hay dust in the nearest irrigation ditch, and, I can only imagine, at least noticed the tractors that were running around sweeping hay. Me, I rode the horses pulling up the stacker, however.

And, I was once visiting poet John Neihardt at the home of his long-time, long-term host, Julius Young. It must have been about 1965 or 1966. After our conversation, as I was leaving, Julius insisted on hauling me back behind a shed to show me his prize, a neat little tractor with all sorts of belly-mount equipment that was absolutely perfect for his acreage. Yeah, yeah, yeah . . . neat tractor. Goofy, though. Not like any tractor I could recall seeing, but then I'd never spent much time looking at tractors. Today I know it was a gorgeous little Allis Chalmers G I would kill for. On that occasion I didn't ask him to start it up, didn't touch it; in fact, I didn't look at it any closer than ten feet. There were all those weeds, and besides, it was just a tractor.

And that's it. I never had anything more than that to do with tractors in the first forty years of my life

Christmas spirit

Celebrating the Yuletide season in style with suitably red lights outlining an International Harvester 1586 in Williamsburg, Massachusetts, in 1993. (Photograph by Paul Rezendes)

than those two brief brushes. But now I had been offered a tractor of my own, so I found a friend with a trailer who was willing to haul whatever it was I had taken as a gift (I had no idea what kind of tractor it might be). We went to the woodlot where the tractor was supposed to be parked, and found it without any trouble. My friend said it was orange, and there it was. Orange, in so far as it had any color. I was a little surprised that it was so large. I don't know what I expected; today I know that this particular machine is not especially large, certainly not in terms of what modern tractors look like. I was a little surprised that it was so old, although I had no idea how old. And I was a little disappointed that it was so battered and, clearly, nonfunctional. I had, I guessed at that point, saved this so-called friend the costs of having the thing hauled to a scrapyard.

My hauling friend suggested that we dump a pint or two of gas in the thing and pop the clutch to see if it might start, so we could drive it onto his trailer instead of hand-winching it. Yeah, sure, Geno, "Start it!!" As if this pile of junk would ever run again! He hooked a chain between the hulk and his pick-up truck, I got into the seat—the first moment I had ever sat on a tractor seat—he pulled, and after a few errors, I figured out where the clutch was, put it into gear—once I figured out where the gears were—and popped the clutch. And after years of sitting there rusting, this machine started. And she didn't just roar, she went. She went up the ramp and onto the trailer. And I sat there on my new tractor, utterly amazed at what just had happened—not just that I was covered with mice poop, wasp nests, dirt, twigs, acorns, and other assorted organic and inorganic trash that had accumulated in that machine over the years and had now blown out all over me. No, I was amazed at the heart of this old girl.

But I'm nowhere close to the love story part yet. At this point, I was just impressed that I had apparently brought off a pretty good bargain. See? I still thought this friend presumed he had palmed off junk on me. I hadn't yet learned even the most basic lesson of Old Iron: THEY RUN!!

But I learned that lesson fairly quickly. Sweet Allis, as she came to be known, sat lonely and cold (but under a canvas cover) down by my cabin by the river for ten or twelve years. But she started every time I turned the crank. When no other vehicle would start

because of the cold—no truck or automobile—Sweet Allis started. Every time. She did her jobs around the farm loyally, but she also became a kind of sports vehicle. I gained a certain amount of fame in town because when I went in to hoo-ha with my buddies at the tavern, I would drive in Sweet Allis and park her directly in front of the tavern, where she sat faithfully, handsomely, waiting for my return—like a good horse or a good dog. Her roar became something of a tradition in town too. Eric, the tavern owner, always had a cold beer waiting on the bar for me when I drove up, usually apologizing that it might have gotten a touch warm, since he had drawn it the moment he heard me start up Sweet Allis . . . a full mile and a half away.

Sweet Allis was—is—a good friend. But this still isn't the part about the mushy love story. I didn't own a set of wrenches, using mostly pliers and a crescent wrench for what little mechanicking I did. I had developed, in fact, some pride in my utter lack of interest and talent for anything to do with engines, machines, vehicles, that sort of thing. To this day I have never greased or changed the oil in one of my automobiles. It's just not what I do. When I thought Sweet Allis needed any sort of attention—she rarely did—or I thought it was about time to give her a lube job or oil change, I took her to the service station in town. I wouldn't have known where to put the grease gun—if I'd have had a grease gun.

I'll spare you the details, but somewhere along the line I picked up another model of the same tractor (as I learned later, an Allis Chalmers WC model, probably produced in 1937). And for some reason, one day I decided to do something on it—fix a broken brake lever, maybe change the oil—something. Why? God only knows, and I use that proper noun deliberately. I cannot help but wonder if this wasn't some sort of divine intervention.

No, this clearly was not a matter of love at first sight. It wasn't even love at 500th sight. Jeez, I had known this machine for two decades! What changed? Why now?! Why did I suddenly see Sweet Allis not as a useful tool, not even as a loyal friend, but as an object of love? I have absolutely no idea . . . none whatsoever. But there it was: I was smitten. Irredeemably, hopelessly in love. Suddenly I wanted to know everything I could about Allis WCs. I wanted to know what makes them run, what keeps them from run-

Amish tractor and team

Many Old Order farmers have strict rules against using motorized farm tractors—but their church does allow them to use motors for farming. Hence, this Lancaster County, Pennsylvania, farmer uses his team to pull a motorized mower. (Photograph by Jerry Irwin)

ning when they don't. I became ever more enchanted by their charm and beauty. . . .

Sweet Allis still sits regally in her own stall in the machine shed. She is still my prize, my first old iron love. I have accumulated a couple dozen more tractors—a mess of WCs, a couple WDs and Cs, a G—but my eye still goes first and best to unstyled WCs, just like Sweet Allis. And while I love the machines I have taken from utter junk to running junk, it is still Sweet Allis I drive to town now and then, still Sweet Allis I pat on the hood as I go in and out of the machine shed every day, still Sweet Allis whose story I tell. Sweet Allis, an old friend turned into a new love who owns my heart.

See what I mean? Beyond logic. It's goofy. It's crazy. Like any love, it's . . . well, it's love.

That is the value of the stories in this remarkable collection. Sure, in reading this book you are going to pick up a little history, a little geography, a hint or two about machinery, mechanisms, and mechanics. But that's not the point. If love is indeed irrational and, therefore, inexplicable, it does nonetheless allow itself to be demonstrated—if not explained—in examples of how it has affected others.

And here we are, with *This Old Tractor*—fifteen vignettes about the curious attraction some people have for rusty, smelly, ugly, outdated, used-up, thrown-out, turned-down, done-in old iron. Tractors like Sweet Allis. Don't expect to learn much in these pages about pistons, hydraulics, agriculture, psychology, or investments in antique machinery. That's not what these stories are about.

These are love stories.

Roger Welsch
Primrose Farm
Dannebrog, Nebraska

This Old Tractor

I first took the wheel of a tractor at age eight, piloting a John Deere from my father's lap. Even today, I remember well the glory of driving that tractor, the feeling of mechanical power and muscular strength in that big green machine, sitting high above a Minnesota cornfield and looking out over the tops of corn stalks for as far as I could see. I have since driven Allis-Chalmers, David Brown, Ford N Series, Farmall, and other tractors, as well as Lamborghini automobiles and Ducati motorcycles, but that first, youthful drive in the John Deere still evokes great memories.

Memories are what this book is all about. For many farmers, the farm tractor is almost a part of the family. Many farmers still remember their first sight of one of the newfangled mechanical mules or their first time behind the wheel of a tractor. And some still remember the day their favorite horse team was traded in for the seemingly cold-blooded steel of machinery as a new way of life came to pass on the family farm.

This book is a treasury of memories—short stories, essays, and reminiscences—devoted to the farm tractor and its role on the family farm. The stories are at times worshipful of a family's beloved "Poppin' Johnny." At other times, they are nothing more than a long, drawn out curse about a Fordson that refused to ever be coaxed into life, remembered vividly, even now, seventy years after the guilty party is long retired to a scrapyard. Whatever the case, all of the stories are nostalgic, sentimental, and sometimes humorous, and all pay homage to the machine that created a revolution in world agriculture.

Many of the essays are written by well-known and respected tractor historians, including Ralph W. Sanders, Randy Leffingwell, Robert N. Pripps, C. H. Wendel, Don Macmillan, and Bill Vossler. Other stories come from tractor collectors and restorers, including Claire D. Scheibe, Gerard W. Rinaldi, and Palmer Fossum.

There are also stories here that are memoirs of farming life, evocative of a time and place—and often of the tractors and other farm machinery that played such an important part in people's lives. These authors include John Hildebrand, Sara De Luca, Patricia Penton Leimbach, Ben Logan, Ed Klimuska, and cartoonist Bob Artley.

Finally, there is a fun piece by Roger Welsch of CBS *Sunday Morning* fame that will make all tractor collectors—and, hopefully, their spouses—laugh at his insights into Old Iron collecting and "rustoration."

The photography and illustrations come from a variety of well-known tractor photographers, including Ralph W. Sanders, Andrew Morland, Randy Leffingwell, John O. Allen, Keith Baum, Jerry Irwin, Andy Kraushaar, Vincent Manocchi, and the late Peter Letourneau. In addition, the Deere & Company's archives provided many valuable historical illustrations. Artist Max E. Neufeldt provided the pen-and-ink drawings of tractors that grace the story openings.

In the end, this book was designed to be part oral history of the farm tractor, part tribute, and part good fun. Enjoy.

Michael Dregni

Ready for work
James G. Cockshutt founded his firm at Brantford, Ontario, in 1877, producing primarily plows in the early years. Jeff Gravert of Central City, Nebraska, restored this Canadian-built 1951 Cockshutt 30 Diesel. Cockshutt and its line of tractors was incorporated into the Oliver Corporation in 1962. (Photograph by Ralph W. Sanders)

Chapter 1

Farewell Horses

"The new-fangled tractors will be the ruination of the farmer because they don't make no manure."
—**Tractor nonbeliever's proverb, 1920s**

Old Dobbin's days were numbered when Henry Ford's first Fordson coughed and sputtered and kicked its way into life. It was the birth of a revolution in farming—and the sign that a way of farm life was coming to an end.

But while many farmers looked to the tractor as their salvation, those same farmers also wiped a tear from their eyes as they said farewell to their team of horses. These stories celebrate the arrival of the general-purpose farm tractor and serve as a requiem for the faithful farm horse.

Workhorses
LARGE PHOTO: *An Amish farmer in Lancaster County, Pennsylvania, still uses his team of workhorses to cultivate crops in the 1990s. (Photograph by Jerry Irwin)*

"How One Case Tractor Replaces 12 Horses"
INSET: *This 1923 Australian brochure from J. I. Case was chock-full of affidavits from farmers pleased with their new methods of power farming. (Peter Letourneau collection)*

Goodbye Horses, Hello Farmall

By Ralph W. Sanders

Ralph Sanders grew up on a central Illinois farm where he had ample opportunity to "exercise" regularly a 1933 Farmall F-12 and a 1948 Farmall C. Helping neighbors bale straw, apply anhydrous ammonia, and shell corn also provided working acquaintances with a Farmall H, Farmall MD, and McCormick W-6.

Ralph became a journalist, working for *Prairie Farmer* and, later, *Successful Farming* magazine. He is the author and photographer of the long-running DuPont *Classic Farm Tractors* calendar, as well as two thorough histories of farm tractors, *Vintage Farm Tractors* and *Vintage International Harvester Tractors*, both published by Voyageur Press.

In this essay, Ralph writes of a momentous day on the family farm—and the epiphany that came to him years later about the day's importance.

I was a small boy of five on the home farm in Illinois when the day came. At breakfast one morning in early spring 1938, my father suggested I help him spread manure that day. I was young enough that it was an honor to "help" Dad with anything—and at that age I had little experience with the tough job that manure loading could be. I remember now, from later experience, it was a job you attached yourself to by grabbing an ash handle whose business end was four steel prongs, and then digging in. Right hand low on the handle for lifting and the left hand high on the handle for control in the throw.

My older brother Jack was in school and my younger brother Jim was not yet three. Jim, although also willing to help Dad, was "needed" to "help" Mother in the house. So I was honored and anxious to be Dad's helper that chilly morning. It's taken me sixty years and some thoughtful reflection to figure out why he needed my help in the barn that day. After all, a five-year-old can't fork much hay-tangled, cattle-packed manure.

While Dad went to the barn and harnessed the team to the old Emerson-Brantingham manure spreader, Mother helped me find and don my coat, hat, and mittens, and I was off to the barn. There in the west driveway, where the feeder cattle fed on the alfalfa hay pitched into the bunks from the hay mow above, was Dad, the team, and the spreader. Dad was already hard at work filling the spreader with great overhanging forkfuls of steaming manure. I helped as best I could, mainly by staying out of his way. I may have even held the horses. They were a gentle pair.

About the time Dad had the spreader mounded

Hello Farmall
The dawn of a new era: a 1937 International Harvester Farmall F-30 narrow-tread. Owner: Don Rimathe of Huxley, Iowa. (Photograph by Ralph W. Sanders)

full, a stranger (to me) came to the barn. He wanted to see the horses work, Dad explained to me later. So sitting side-by-side on the spreader seat, Dad and I drove to the field south of the barn, put the spreader in gear with the lever beside the seat, adjusted the speed of the unloading apron with the other lever, and began to spread out the load.

All this time the stranger walked alongside and carefully watched the horses as they plodded along, leaning well into the harness as they pulled the heavy spreader and its spinning beater. It was a quiet scene with only the rhythmic metallic clanks of the ratchet that moved the apron and the whir of the spreader beaters as they tore through the manure and flung it randomly to the rear. The team knew their job. They pulled the load steadily without protest and with only clucks of encouragement from Dad.

I must have gotten cold and headed to the house once we got back to the barn, since I have no recollection of the conversation that must have ensued between Dad and the stranger. I certainly would have perked up my ears and paid attention had I known what they were talking about.

I had forgotten the events of that morning until one afternoon days later when I heard a laboring truck shifting through its gears coming up our long gravel driveway. I was supposed to be taking a nap (mandatory until the age of six at the Sanders farm) but I had to investigate. When I looked out of the second floor window of "the boy's room" to the driveway below, I saw a stock-rack-equipped truck hauling a gray tractor with red steel wheels. Squeezed in beside the front of the tractor was a cultivator and some other implement. Could that tractor be ours or was the driver just lost and looking for another farm?

Obedient son that I was, I stayed in the bedroom pretending to nap. Sometime later the truck started again and when I peeked down as it passed the house on its way out the lane, the story began to fall into place. Even a five-year-old could figure out most of it. Our last team had been loaded into the truck and our horses were leaving the farm. The tractor had been unloaded—it was staying!

Our "new" tractor was a five-year-old F-12 Farmall on steel wheels with a two-row front-mounted cultivator and a rear-mounted sickle-bar mower. Dad had traded the last team—the one he had kept for cultivating corn—on the F-12. The stranger (probably the tractor dealer or his salesman) that had watched the horses spread manure just wanted to see them work to insure their soundness before making the deal on the tractor. Dad was probably just as cautious about negotiating a deal with return privileges on the tractor in case it didn't work out.

Dad took some good-natured ribbing about the swap from my Uncle Bain, mother's brother. "John," he said, "you shouldn't have traded your last horses for a tractor. Now you're going to raise three sons that won't know how to harness a team." Convinced he had done the right thing, Dad answered laconically, "Yes, Bain, but I never learned to yoke oxen, and I seem to be getting by."

By the time I was ten, the same age as the F-12, it had been equipped with Montgomery Ward Riverside knob-tread rubber tires and a high gear that gave it a blistering top speed of 5 mph (8 km/h)—if you pulled hard enough on the notched throttle rod. The F-12 tractor became "my" tractor when my legs were long enough that I could push in the clutch without sliding all the way off the seat.

With it I could do a lot of the light tractor work including spike-tooth harrowing-down of rough spring-plowed ground. With a four-section harrow, that was sometimes a heavy pull. Plowing with the F-12 and a two-fourteen (35-cm) plow was an experience. The plow was too big for the tractor—two twelve-inch (30-cm) bottoms would have been better.

Dad used sweet clover as the legume interplanted in the small grain in the crop rotation. The sweet clover was often pastured when it was held over for a year in the corn, soybeans, wheat, or oats on a four-year crop rotation. Plowing under the rank sweet clover with the F-12 provided the spectacle of getting stuck on every cow pie the knobby-tired left wheel encountered. Only by using the hand brakes on that side to transfer power to the right wheel could I get the rig moving again. Stubble and pasture clipping with the mounted mower was fun. The F-12 let you cut square corners without slowing down.

As we grew up with the tractor one of our tests of our young manhood was to have the strength to "spin" (or continuously turn) the starting crank. We three Sanders boys could soon spin the crank at will. We were either getting stronger or the tractor was getting weaker and needed a ring job.

Dad always drove the tractor to plant and cultivate corn, both critical operations. My brothers and I lacked the needed skills to plant checkrowed corn and were short of the back strength needed to manually lift the F-12's lever-operated cultivator.

We used the hardy little F-12 tractor through World War II. It got some relief about 1944 when Dad added a Ford-Ferguson 2N to our three-tractor fleet. Heavy tillage was done with a four-plow gasoline Caterpillar.

The gray F-12 (looking black by then) was traded for a shiny new red Farmall C about 1948. With its hydraulic implement lift, starter, lights, ease of driving, good seat, and superior visibility, the C was a pleasure to operate. During my last three years in high school and my first two years of college, I cultivated a lot of corn on the farm each summer with the Farmall C. Unlike the horses, the C was never traded; it's still on the farm where it helps do chores for my older brother Jack.

And what has been finally revealed to me after sixty years? Not only was my father anxious to share his time with me as a boy of five that early spring morning, but he also wanted me to witness a great change that was occurring on the farm in our lifetimes, that of the passing of horses from use on farms. I didn't figure it out in time to thank him for that. But I will always be grateful I was there with him that day to share the experience.

"One Man Can Farm More Land . . ."

BOTH PHOTOS: *The Moline Plow Company of Moline, Illinois, offered the Universal tractor from 1915 through 1923 as a gasoline-powered replacement for the feed-driven horse of flesh and blood. As Moline advertisements of the day boasted, "One Man has power at his command equal to five horses, capable of doing the work of seven horses owing to its greater speed and endurance." (Photograph from Minnesota Historical Society collection; ad from the Michael Dregni collection)*

OLD MAG
By J. Edward Tufft, *Successful Farming*, 1918

Old Mag is so shopworn and old, I sometimes think she should be sold to Dage, the garbage man; she'd do for him all right, I know—he'd pay me fifteen bones or so, and use her on his van. He never overworks his horse, has no occasion to, of course, and feeds real well, I hear. I need the fifteen dollars too. To meet a note that's coming due some later in the year. Old Mag's front knees are badly sprung, she has a ringbone, badly rung, her wind is out of key; it's hard for her to chew her hay, I grind and soak her feed each day—she is no use to me! But Mag was born on this old farm, for years she worked just like a charm—some sixteen years at least; she was old Dolly's second colt, was never known to balk or bolt—she's been an honest beast! When'er the women used a horse they always took Old Mag, of course, she was so safe and sane, and yet when I had call for speed I always took the same old steed and let her have the rein. Ben, Barney, Pudge, Skylark and Bay, the five best nags I have today, are all her sons, all five; they have their mother's gait and step, her gentle nature and her pep— the best old horse alive! So, when I take a second thought I fear Old Mag can not be bought for fifteen dollars yet,— and add five hundred more to that, I'd turn it down as quick as scat; I surely would, Old Pet!

The Iron Horse

The 1921 Samson Iron Horse tractor was aptly—and carefully—named. It was designed by the Samson Iron Works of Stockton, California, to have many qualities of the horse, including optional rein controls and four-wheel drive in place of the horse's four legs. The name was designed to comfort farmers skeptical about switching to power farming. Other tractors also offered rein drive in the early years, including the well-named Rein Drive Tractor of Toronto, Ontario. This restored Iron Horse is driven by Eldon Coates of Zwingle, Iowa. (Photograph by Ralph W. Sanders)

Memories of a Former Kid
Bob Artley

For several decades now, artist Bob Artley has collected his reminiscences of farm life into a syndicated cartoon series entitled "Memories of a Former Kid" that originated from the *Worthington Daily Globe* in Worthington, Minnesota. His drawings and essays have also been collected into several books, including *Memories of a Former Kid, Cartoons II,* and *A Book of Chores As Remembered by a Former Kid.*

These four cartoons recall the day when the tractor—in this case, a Fordson—came to stay on the Artley farm and soon became part of the family.

Sunrise

Gasoline-powered tractors brought a new era of farm power to American, Canadian, and European farms, such as this farm in Lancaster County, Pennsylvania. (Photograph by Jerry Irwin)

FAREWELL OLD DOBBIN
By Harry Mount of Ohio, 1918

Weather conditions, farm labor, and the price of good farm horses are such that the tractor is a coming necessity. I say coming necessity because farm labor and the price of good farm horses after the war in Europe is over will be so high that the American farmer will have most of his work to do alone. It is then that factories will reap their harvest with the farmer close behind, providing he can get machinery such as the tractor that will take the place of hired help and horses.

Better Farming
With
Better Tractors

J.I. Case Threshing Machine Company
INCORPORATED
Racine, Wisconsin, U.S.A.

Tractors

By Ben Logan

Novelist and filmmaker Ben Logan lives in New York City, although he remains rooted to the southwestern Wisconsin farm where he grew up. As he writes at the start of his colorful memoir of his family's farm, *The Land Remembers*, "Once you have lived on the land, been a partner with its moods, secrets, and seasons, you cannot leave. The living land remembers, touching you in unguarded moments, saying, 'I am here. You are part of me.'"

In this chapter from Ben's memoir, he describes his yearning for a tractor after seeing a Fordson on a friend's acreage in the 1920s. This story underscores the farmer's ambivalence toward the newfangled tractor: part desire for the mechanical mule, part fear that it would symbolize the end to a way of life.

One summer when I was about nine I fell in love with tractors. It began with a Sunday visit of the whole family to friends who lived in a little valley branching off from the Kickapoo River. There was a boy my age named Don and an older boy named George. They also had two sisters and I didn't, so I was interested in sisters. But they told me sisters were a pain, and I took their word for it.

I envied Don and George even before they got a tractor. A little creek ran practically through their barnyard, the riffles filling the place with the sound of water and the feel of a long lazy summer day. There were suckers and chubs in the pools, waiting to be caught, and slippery mud puppies in the banks, looking like foot-long dinosaurs.

And on the steep hillside above the stream was a giant prostrate juniper that made a great ground-hugging circle of dark green. I had never seen a tree before that grew out along the ground instead of up toward the sky. It had decided to be different, and

was a fairy ring that invited me to race around it in the short grass of the hillside until I dropped to the warm ground, panting and dizzy, breathing in the rich pungence of the juniper, feeling the hot sun beating down on me.

Those people had those two things, and they had a tractor. On this particular day we walked, Don and George and I, up the narrow valley along the singing creek to find the tractor. Grasshoppers flew up ahead of us, some of them landing in the water. We stopped to look down at a grasshopper thrashing in the middle of a quiet pool, sending out little waves in a perfect series of rings that vanished at the edge.

We argued awhile about whether the rings would ever end. If the pool were big enough, would they go on forever, maybe even after the three of us were dead? If the whole world were water, would the grasshopper waves go clear around it and meet on the other side? And where would that be? In the China Sea, maybe?

Then we argued about the grasshopper's swimming ability. For me to float and thrash my arms at the same time was a newly discovered and death-defying

"Better Farming with Better Tractors"
J. I. Case's full line brochure from the dawn of the 1920s offered everything from steamers to gas-powered tractors—as well as Case automobiles—and warned the horse stalwarts that "Power is the one big factor within the farmer's control that determines the productivity of the soil." (Peter Letourneau collection)

accomplishment. "He's swimming," I said.

"He's trying to swim," said Don.

We waited for George's opinion. He frowned down at the struggling grasshopper. "He's floating because he can't sink even if he wants to. He's trying to walk, like he was still up here in the field."

All at once the grasshopper wasn't doing any of those things. There was a little swirl, a sucking, crunching sound, and the grasshopper was gone. A bigger series of waves spread to the edge of the pool.

"He can too sink," said Don.

George got a patient, older-brother look. "He didn't sink. He was sunk. One of three things happened. A turtle got him, a trout got him, or a chub got him."

"Sometimes you sound just like a goddamned sister," Don said.

"You're not supposed to say goddamn," George said.

"You just said it."

"That was only to tell you not to say it."

"Just the same you said it. And if you tell that I said it, I can tell that you said it, too. Anyways what about a frog?"

"I don't think frogs eat grasshoppers," George said.

During all this we chased down another grasshopper and threw him in the water. He drifted slowly downstream. Nothing happened.

"Let's go see the tractor," I said.

It was a Fordson with cleated steel wheels, a steering wheel of wood and iron, and a crank hanging down in front, the same as a Model T. It smelled of new paint, grease, and gasoline, and it crouched there in the hayfield, ready to spring into life. I walked around and around that tractor, seeing the heat waves dance up from the broad hood, moving in to touch it sometimes, then moving back and walking around again.

"How do you start it?" I asked.

"We can't do that," Don said.

For some reason we were both whispering.

George was looking back down the creek. A bend in the valley hid us from the farm buildings. George turned around and looked at Don. "Look, when Papa was using it up here yesterday, could you hear it? At the house?"

Don swallowed. "I don't think so."

George smiled. "Tell you what, little brother, if you won't tell I started it, I won't tell you said

goddamn. O.K.?"

"O.K," Don said. "I won't even tell you said goddamn twice."

George fiddled a minute with levers and knobs. Then he went around front and started cranking. The engine wheezed and coughed a couple times, smoke came out of the exhaust pipe, and then it started and settled into a steady roar. George climbed up to the seat, throttled it down, got it into gear, and ran it forward and back a couple of times. Then he stopped and waved me toward him. "Want to steer it?" he yelled.

I didn't know if I wanted to or not, but he reached down and helped me up to the seat. He got it going and stood behind me while I steered that vibrating monster in a slow circle.

George shut it off. I was holding on to the wheel so hard I couldn't let go. Slowly the sound of the creek and the flying bees came back. I finally climbed down to the ground. A bell was ringing.

"That's dinner," Don said.

We raced through the sweet-smelling hay, sending the grasshoppers, bumblebees, and honeybees sailing off in all directions.

That afternoon, driving back up to the ridge, I started talking about the tractor.

"You boys didn't start it up, did you?" Mother asked.

While I was trying to think my way out of that, Father saved me. He looked at Mother and said, "If you want a boy to make a habit of speaking the truth, there's some things you don't ask."

I wanted to reach across the seat of the Model T and hug Father, but then I thought about how that might say we had started the tractor. The moment of warmth passed.

Mother sighed. I knew exactly what she was thinking. Any time a bunch of women got together they talked about tractors as if they were some kind of monsters that roamed the country eating people. Those women had all the news for a hundred miles around about tip-overs, broken arms from cranking, fingers cut off in gears, and some poor man over in Iowa so chopped up and scattered it wasn't even worth while to buy a coffin. Some of it was true, of course. There was no arguing with the fact that one of our neighbors got confused and sat up there on the tractor seat pulling back on the wheel, yelling "Whoa," and drove right out through the end of the machine

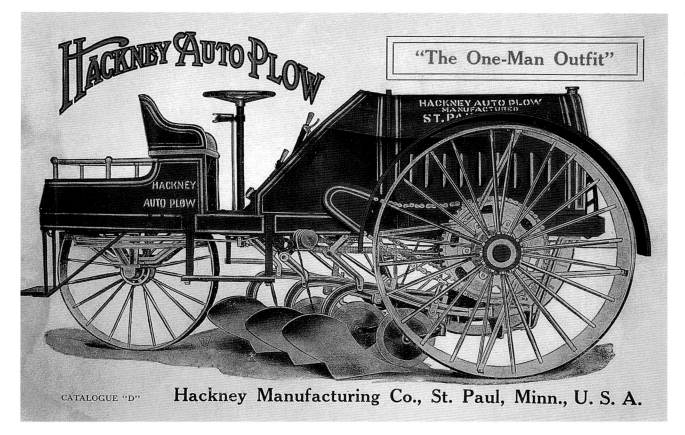

HACKNEY AUTO PLOW

"The One-Man Outfit"

HACKNEY AUTO PLOW MANUFACTURED ST. PA...

HACKNEY AUTO PLOW

CATALOGUE "D"   Hackney Manufacturing Co., St. Paul, Minn., U. S. A.

"The One-Man Outfit"

Fledgling tractor companies throughout North America and Europe crafted various powered machines to lift the yoke from the horse and place it on mechanized horsepower. The Hackney Auto-Plow from St. Paul, Minnesota, was one such contraption introduced in 1911 and built until 1918. The Auto-Plow featured a design based on the automobiles of the day and mounted with three underslung plows. Taking the automobile-plow concept a step further was the Sylvester Auto Thresher from Sylvester Manufacturing Company of Lindsay, Ontario; the Auto Thresher was a self-propelled thresher introduced in 1907 that could also do heavy drawbar work. (Minnesota Historical Society collection)

PLOUGHMEN WHO NEEDED FINGER-BOARD AND COMPASS
By A. C. Wood of Ontario, Canada, 1918

I knew a young Englishman in my homesteading days out West who always put up a stake at the end of his furrows. I asked him one day why he did this and he said it was to assist him in finding his way back to the place he started from. He was ploughing with oxen and on prairie that had some stones and wolf-willow roots. Looking at his work I did not wonder further about his using guiding stakes, because the ploughed ground looked as if an insane elephant had been rooting up the sod with its tusks. That ploughman couldn't tell whether he was going or coming—

that's why he had a finger-board to show him the proper point of the compass to head for.

They used to tell a story out West about a young emigrant who was from a big city and who knew nothing about ploughing. They said he had a compass fastened to the beam of his breaking plough because when he started out with a furrow there was grave danger of his getting lost on the prairie. I don't present this as unadulterated truth but I've heard it told by those breezy, free and sometimes careless of fact, local history-makers on the plains.

Waterloo Boy, then and now

BOTH PHOTOS: *With the inventive mind of engineer John Froelich at the helm, the Waterloo Gasoline Engine Company of Waterloo, Iowa, was a pioneer in developing gas tractors. The Waterloo Boy tractor made its debut in about 1912, and was refined and updated through 1924. The tractor's success spurred Deere & Company to buy the firm in 1918, so that Deere could sell a tractor of its own to pull Deere plows. This restored 1920 Model N is owned by Don Wolf. (Photograph by Andrew Morland; ad from the Michael Dregni collection)*

A FIRST DAY AT THE PLOUGH
By A. C. Wood of Ontario, Canada, 1918

Ploughing on our farm was one of the exact arts. It had to be done well or somebody would lose his job, and I knew this as one sunny morning I was turned loose into and instructed to turn over the summer fallow of several acres. I had never set out alone to plough before but had been allowed to hold the plough a few rounds on occasion.

I felt I was one of the lords of creation that morning as I hitched my team to that most ancient of all the implements of earth and set forth to acquire knowledge in the art of turning furrows. I'd decided that I'd be a hero of the plough, that is, that I'd win prizes at the township, county and, perhaps, provincial ploughing matches.

. . . I freely admit that my first furrows were irregular and somewhat resembled the old cow path that ran crooked to the wood. My plough bumped into many stones and it seemed to me that I was hit on both sides at once by those plough handles at times. The dew of duty—as the poet terms it—was on my brow. I was perspiring, yes, just plain sweating. It was a hot and dusty job but all my troubles vanished when along about the middle of the forenoon my father came to investigate, and informed me that, for a beginner, in the manly art of turning furrows, I was doing very well indeed.

At dinner that first day at the plough I found myself gripping my knife and fork as if I still had hold of the plough handles. I was terribly in earnest and I remember that I related to my mother my adventures in the broad field of agriculture with some pride.

"But you're not going to be a farmer, my son," she said with a kindly smile. You see my mother's ambition was that I should be a minister, and perhaps, she felt I was becoming too enamoured of the work of making parallel straight marks on the surface of the earth. I write "parallel" with fear and trembling. Some reader may have seen me plough at some time or other.

I recall, too, that during the afternoon I discussed with a neighbour, while leaning on the line fence, the most approved methods of disposing of Canada thistles and other pestiferous weeds. Getting along fast, wasn't I?

Yes, indeed, the day he goes forth to plough for the first time is the beginning of a new era—a momentous occasion—in the life of a farmer's son.

Automobile plow
Early tractors were often built around the state-of-the-art automobile designs of the time, and this unidentified tractor prototype from Minneapolis, Minnesota, in the 1910s was typical of the attempts to mesh car with plow. Minneapolis–St. Paul was once one of the tractor manufacturing capitals of the world, featuring numerous makers—from the Toro Manufacturing Company to the Minneapolis-Moline Company. (Minnesota Historical Society collection)

shed.

I read about tractors in the farm magazines that summer and talked about them until everybody was disgusted with me. The trouble was nobody else got excited about them except maybe Mother and Lyle, and they were on the other side. Lee liked the idea of getting the work done faster. Junior would have liked another engine to tinker with. Laurance dismissed the whole idea with such older-brother phrases as "just not a practical possibility."

Just mention the word tractor to Mother and she could see one tipping over, wiping out a whole family. Father listened to the talk and smiled, saying very little.

Lyle was the antitractor spokesman. I would bring up the subject and then it would go something like this:

"We don't raise gasoline. We raise hay. Ever try feeding hay to a tractor?"

"But a tractor doesn't eat hay when it isn't working."

"Doesn't make any manure either."

"But a tractor would save a lot of time."

"Sure, and what happens when you need a new one? We going to take the old one next door and breed it to a neighbor's tractor and wait for it to have a little tractor?"

It was no use. Lyle always got the last word.

Late that summer I was with Father when he stopped to talk to an old man named Abe who had a little farm out near the end of the ridge. Abe was standing at the edge of a hayfield watching a red tractor and a two-bottom plow roar across the field.

"Never thought I'd see a tractor on your land," Father said.

"Had to get one. My boy wouldn't stay with me otherwise. He's the last one I got. Damn it, Sam, a man gets old."

Abe picked up a clod of dirt and slowly crumbled it between his fingers. "I broke this land. This was the first field. I cut off the timber, grubbed out the brush. I put an old breaking plow behind three of the best horses that ever lived. I followed that plow around this field, dodging stumps, turning up rocks bigger than a man could lift. And goddammit, Sam, last year a man from the government was out here telling me I shouldn't be farming this hillside."

"You mean the county agent?" Father asked.

"Hell, I don't know. Could've been. It was one of those government men from somewhere. I told him it was the closest thing to a level field I got. Hell, he might as well tell me I should never made a living all these years."

The tractor roared by us in a cloud of smoke and dust, throwing up two fourteen-inch furrows of sod. Abe's son—I guess he must have been about twenty-five—waved down to us. He had a smile going that just about took up his whole face.

"He's got a glory all right," Abe said. "I had one, too. Mine was making this farm out of nothing. But that contraption—that's his glory."

"Well, things change," Father said in that way he had sometimes of just saying enough to keep somebody else talking.

Abe nodded. "Things change all right. That don't mean I have to like it. Seems to me a tractor gets a man up in the air too high. I figure I got to be down on the ground where I can get dirt on my hands and get the smell of it. I got to walk and get the feel of it under me. Then I can say when it's too wet or too dry. I can say what it needs. You can't tell me that boy of mine's going to know all that going across a field hell bent for election way up there on a tractor."

We left him there with a handful of earth running through his fingers, his eyes locked on the red tractor.

We got in the car. I was very quiet. Father looked at me. "What's the matter?"

It isn't easy when you're nine—or any age—to say you've thought of a man as being old and foolish and have suddenly found out he's not only not foolish but almost a poet of some kind.

"I didn't know he felt like that," I said.

Father nodded. "Still think we should have a tractor?"

I could feel the steering wheel of that Fordson jerking against my hands. I could smell the gasoline and hot oil smells and hear the roar of power I had commanded from way up on that swaying seat. I still wanted a tractor. But it wasn't the same.

"Not as much," I said. Father smiled.

Motor Cultivator

ABOVE: *In the 1910s, International Harvester had a vision of the future of farming: small, lightweight tractors that could be operated by one farmer and were inexpensive enough that they would replace the horse. In 1917, the firm introduced the Motor Cultivator, but the design was top heavy, ungainly, and proved to be short lived, lasting only until 1920. But from this machine would grow the seeds of the famous Farmall. Similar motor cultivators were offered by the Savoie-Guay Company of Plessisville, Quebec, whose One-Man Motor Plow was introduced in 1915. Owner: Wes Stratman of Pueblo, Colorado; the driver is Bill Splinter of Lincoln, Nebraska. (Photograph by Ralph W. Sanders)*

Farming revolution

RIGHT: *International Harvester's Farmall signified a revolution in farming when it made its debut in 1924. The new general-purpose row-crop machine featured adjustable tread width and a power takeoff. It was reliable, lightweight, and affordable. This Farmall Regular was painted in the tractor's original gray before the famous Farmall Red became the standard color in 1936. (Photograph by Andrew Morland)*

DOBBIN'S ETERNAL SLUMBERS
From a Holt Manufacturing Company
advertisement, circa 1900s

The horse is sliding off the map;
his friends at last admit it.
He'll hang around a while mayhap,
but soon he'll have to quit.

For things propelled with gasoline
increase each day in numbers,
And Dobbin leaves this earthly scene
for his eternal slumbers.

MORE TIME TO SMOKE AND REST
From a horse advocacy advertisement, 1915

I'll let my neighbor fret and stew
about the things his tractor'll do;
I'll take old Dan and Kate and Ned,
and hitch them to a plow instead.
Let neighbor plow with his machine
and raise his with gasoline;
My way of farming is the best;
I have more time to smoke and rest.

"The Universal Tractor"

LEFT: *Following its debut in 1917, Henry Ford's Fordson trac-tor was so ubiquitous on farms that the firm advertised on the cover of* Farm Mechanics *magazine in 1924 that "Over 75% of all tractors on American farms are Fordsons." The same percentage probably held true for Canadian farms— and was perhaps higher on farms in Great Britain. (Robert N. Pripps collection)*

Bigger is better

Most tractors were big in the 1910s, before Henry Ford's Fordson arrived on the scene. The big tractors were naturally expensive, and so were affordable only to farmers with large acreages, which required the power of the big tractor to pull large plows and other implements. This monstrous 1910 Pioneer 30/60 from the Pioneer Tractor Manufacturing Company of Winona, Minnesota, was typical of the giants that plowed the earth in the pioneering days of the gas tractor. Gigantic tractors have had a revival in recent decades on large farm operations. The mammoth four-wheel drive articulated tractors, built starting in 1966 by the Versatile Manufacturing Company of Winnipeg, Manitoba, and the Steiger company of Fargo, North Dakota, serve much the same purpose as the Pioneer did in its day. Owner: Irvin King of Artesian, South Dakota. (Photograph by Ralph W. Sanders)

Lightning Strike

By Randy Leffingwell

Photographer and writer Randy Leffingwell is known and respected around the globe for his detailed chronicles of farm tractors and his eloquent photographs of old machinery that speak volumes about their stories. He is the author of numerous books, including *The American Farm Tractor*, *John Deere Farm Tractors*, *Caterpillar*, *Classic Farm Tractors*, *Farm Tractors: A Living History*, and more.

During his travels across North America while compiling his first tractor book, Randy met retired Denison, Iowa, farmer Ray Pollock and his 1939 McCormick-Deering Farmall F-20. Both Pollock and the Farmall had a story to tell about the end of horse farming and the dawn of the age of tractors.

"I've never in my life bought a new tractor, never even owned one close to new," Ray Pollock says with a touch of finality. After more than a half century of farming in western Iowa, Pollock has retired, so the likelihood of his buying something new now is remote.

"I bought that F-20 there in 1948. It was a 1939 model and all I ever did to it was grind the valves about ten years ago. You don't need all this high-priced stuff. There's no advantage. These young people starting out haven't got a clue."

Pollock was born in 1915, the third of six children. When he was barely fourteen, the stock market crashed. It was another three years, until Ray was seventeen, before the real depths of the Great Depression hit western Iowa. He was old enough to understand what was happening around him, to his family and their friends.

"Times were tough. Things were real bad. Nobody had anything: no money, no food. Hogs sold for three cents a pound, corn was a dime a bushel. A farmer could rent a farm for, say, ten dollars an acre. Didn't cost much more than that to buy. Except there was no money. City folks couldn't buy the food and farmers couldn't pay their rents or mortgages. You farmed what you had with what you had. There was no way we could go out and buy anything, let alone a tractor."

Pollock, his parents, brothers, and sisters survived the hard times, but the clarity of their memories colored their view of the future. Pollock learned the lessons of careful spending, of husbanding resources against the next hard time.

"I farmed with horses. That F-20 tractor was quite an improvement, you know. You gotta understand, with horses, everything takes time. By the time you harness up your five horses, well, it takes quite a while. You gotta let them rest at the end of each row. And then you gotta bring them in at noon, unhitch 'em, feed 'em, and get 'em watered. Then you can eat. Then back out, and work 'til near dark and when you come in, it's the same old thing over again. Day after day. It's really quite a bit of work. We did ten, sometimes twelve, acres in a day. Really moving. That's including the time to come in for dinner and going

Farmall at sunset

Ray Pollock's 1939 McCormick-Deering Farmall F-20 as it was when Ray retired from farming. (Photograph by Randy Leffingwell)

Working pals
Ray Pollock sits in the saddle of his 1939 McCormick-Deering Farmall F-20. The duo have worked many a season together. (Photograph by Randy Leffingwell)

back out midday.

"Of course, I always had outlaws, too. Real jug-heads. I didn't have good horses, well-trained ones. Couldn't afford them. Mine would as soon kick your head in or run away as work for you."

Keeping horses was work, too. They ate up as much as a fifth of Pollock's crop. They needed shoes and care. Their tack required attention. Even then, things happened that no one could foresee, that no one could control.

"In one single day, I lost three of those horses to lightning. Right out there in the field. No time to unhitch and get 'em to cover, to the barn. I was plow-ing and planting. And now I was down to just two horses. That's the only reason I even bought that trac-tor. I wasn't in any hurry to get one. I just had to get my seed into the ground.

"That Farmall was the first tractor I ever bought. But it made quite a difference, I'll tell you. With the hired man, with the F-20, we plowed all eighty acres in just four days, pulling two sixteen-inch plows. And harrowed it. All of that in just four days. That's maybe two weeks with the horses."

For the next forty-eight years, with time out only for the valve job, that tractor and Ray Pollock oper-ated the farm every day. In 1995, shortly before his eightieth birthday, Ray's son, Bob, finally got him to retire. Bob, a scrap-metal dealer, spirited his father's old Farmall away, but not to the boneyards.

On Ray's birthday, Bob, who is also an antique trac-tor collector, presented his father with the F-20, com-pletely restored.

Horse power

ABOVE: *Even though farmers were retiring their horse teams in favor of gasoline-powered tractors, horses could still be counted on to help out when the going got rough. When this Heider tractor got bogged down while plowing, the farmers harnessed up their retired team and put them to work, adding "horse" power to the tractor. The Heider was built by the Heider Manufacturing Company of Carroll, Iowa, from 1911 to 1927. (Photograph by J. C. Allen and Son)*

"The Future of the Airship in Agriculture"

LEFT: *Anything seemed possible with the revolution in technology following the turn of the century. This cartoon may have been half satire, half wishful thinking, but either way, the cartoonist certainly saw the farm tractor as having a short future ahead of it, given the recent advances in dirigibles. (Gale C. Frost collection)*

Evidence of success

Left: *This 1918 brochure for the Staude Mak-a-Tractor from the E. G. Staude Manufacturing Company of St. Paul, Minnesota, featured signed and notarized affidavits from 363 farmers throughout the United States and Canada lauding the firm's conversion kit that turned the everyday automobile into an iron-willed farm tractor. Such conversion kits were common in the 1910s and 1920s; a kit was even available for the Ford Model T and A cars through the famous Sears, Roebuck & Company mail-order catalog. (Minnesota Historical Society collection)*

THE OIL TRACTOR ON THE SMALL FARM
By Ralph P. Clarkson, *Practical Talks on Farm Engineering*, 1915

While it is certain that the horse can never be entirely dispensed with on the small farm, the light-weight oil tractor of from six to thirty-five horsepower capacity is destined to relieve him of much of the hard work which he does but slowly and which wears him out in the doing. In many places where a horse is valuable the tractor cannot be used, but the decreased cost per acre of farming with the small tractor over that incurred when using horses; the fact that the tractor enables the farmer to do without help at just the time when help is scarce; the fact that when idle the tractor costs nothing to keep; that it requires no rest even on hot days, but, in emergencies, can be used all day and, with lights, work continued after dark; that, being small, it is economical in doing many things besides plowing—can, in fact, do all that a portable engine can do and, besides, propel itself where-ever it is wanted; all these advantages mean more money to the small farmer using such power. He is facing a new era in agriculture. His land, in many cases, has been so abused in the past by the continuous growth of crops without fertilization that it will require hereafter as much plant food put into the soil as is taken out in the crops. This means an added amount of work each year which must be done at certain times. Labour is no longer cheap, and satisfactory farm help is hard to get at any price.

The average work day of a farm horse the year round is only from three to four hours. Yet he must be fed the whole year at a cost averaging, perhaps, $100 for the twelve months. It may not be in cash, but in food that would sell for such an amount if there were no horse. His field of work is limited. Most of the small machinery which runs by belt power is not satisfactorily operated by either a horse sweep or a treadmill, while feed cutters, silo fillers, threshers, and similar machines are too heavy for the horse to handle. His speed on the road under load is very limited, as is his pulling power. The time taken in his care, the repairs to harnesses, the hitching and unhitching several times daily, allowing rest when work is waiting, are all features which raise the operating cost of a horse to a high amount per hour of work he does. On the other hand, the small tractor can be worked continuously every day to plow, harrow, drill, disc, harvest, haul, thresh, run small machines or the largest apparatus, and when it is not needed the power is immediately shut off and costs of operation cease.

Tractor and truck cousins
ABOVE: *The great International Harvester offered its 8/16 tractor in the 1910s, which was built using components from IH's famous Model G truck. The vehicles shared a similar four-cylinder engine and other components. This 1919 VB Series 8/16 was restored by owner Merrill Sheets of Delaware, Ohio. (Photograph by Ralph W. Sanders)*

Johnny Popper

Lightweight tractors came to rule the roost in the 1920s, making big tractors obsolete almost overnight. Among the best were the Fordson, Farmall, and the new line of two-cylinder tractors from Deere & Company of Moline, Illinois. This Model A, pictured in 1937, was the flagship of the "Johnny Popper" line and was popular throughout the United States and Canada. (Deere & Company archives)

FORDSON PROBLEMS
By Gerald Robbins, 1930

My first tractor was a Fordson. The previous owner had installed long spade lugs on the wheels in an effort to increase the traction. These lugs absorbed most of the drawbar power that the worm drive didn't take. I had a breaker plow that the Fordson just could not handle.

Later, I made a tractor using a Model A Ford truck rear axle, two transmissions in series, and a Model A engine. I adapted a set of donut rubber tires and wheels to the machine. This home-made tractor pulled the breaker plow with ease. It would also work all day on five or six gallons of gas, while the Fordson would use as much as twenty-five gallons of kerosene doing the same work.

Power for the farm

The Turner Manufacturing Company of Port Washington, Wisconsin, offered its well-respected Simplicity tractor from 1915 through 1920. The firm later built garden tractors for Montgomery Ward and the Allis-Chalmers Company of Milwaukee, Wisconsin, before being bought out by Allis in 1965. Owners: Harvey Jongeling (left) and Ken Hoogestraat of Chancellor, South Dakota. (Photograph by Ralph W. Sanders)

TRACTOR REPLACES HORSES
By Farmer Marsteller of Indiana, 1918

We have been able to do away with about four extra horses that we just used to get the crops in the spring, and then consumed feed the rest of the year. Our two hands each worked three horses to a plow and had to rest the teams often, as the ground plowed hard, while I took the tractor and plowed right along, and believe I did as much work as three men and nine horses. The tractor helps to get the crops in on time and saves lots of hard work on the horses and men in the spring and is very good for plowing in the fall when it is so hot and dry and you can plow the ground deeper than you have been used to doing.

Of course I do not believe the tractor will ever entirely take the place of horses on the farm, but it will do lots of hard work that the horse is not able to work at steady.

Chapter 2

A Part of the Family

"Farmalls serve their owners by supplying ready power for the thousand and one odd jobs—hauling loads, stretching fence, moving hog and hen houses, sawing wood, pumping water—the doing of which keeps cash in the family purse and makes farm life more interesting and enjoyable."
—International Harvester *The Farmall Family* brochure, 1940s

For many farmers, a tractor became a part of the family. They worked with their tractor from sunup to sundown, through rain, snow, and heat, and repaired the tractor when it broke down. Farmers all but invited the family tractor to the table for Thanksgiving supper.

These stories fondly tell of fine tractors that have come and gone—and more than a few that are still around today.

Lunchtime
LARGE PHOTO: *While Dad eats his lunch, Junior and Spot pretend they are piloting the family's "Poppin' Johnny" in this painting by artist Walter Haskell Hinton for Deere & Company. Deere's early two-cylinder tractors were known variously as "Poppin' Johnnies" or "Johnny Poppers," as the engine's sound was so distinctive; farm wives could tell from the tone of the engine when their husbands had idled down the tractor to come in for supper. (Deere & Company archives)*

Hot date
INSET: *A young couple tries out the ergonomics of the latest in tractor offerings at the Minnesota State Fair in the 1930s. (Minnesota State Fair collection)*

Recollections

By C. H. Wendel

Chuck Wendel is without doubt one of the most famous tractor historians in the world. He was also a pioneer in writing about the farm tractor's history, a job which has taken him through the United States, Canada, and Europe. He has authored almost thirty books, several of which will be recognized by many a tractor fan: the famous *Encyclopedia of American Farm Tractors*, *Massey Tractors* covering Canada's finest, *150 Years of J. I. Case*, *150 Years of International Harvester*, *The Allis-Chalmers Story*, *Unusual Vintage Tractors*, and many more.

In these recollections, Chuck shares some favorite farm tractor yarns about farm people and their tractors.

My Dad had a particular aversion to Fordson tractors. Once when I was about fourteen or fifteen, there was an old Fordson in the neighborhood that interested me. The owner said I could have it for $10. I asked my Dad about it, and he informed me he "wouldn't give a lead nickel for one."

It all went back to the 1920s, when my dad was hired out to a local farmer. This fellow had a Fordson as part of his farm power arsenal, and one morning he told my Dad that he had to be gone for awhile, so that when the chores were done, Dad could take the Fordson out to plow. About ten o'clock, the fellow returned, and there was my Dad, still cranking the Fordson. He got it to pop once or twice, but that was all, and after a couple hours of this, he was almost worn out.

The old fellow walked up to the crank, pulled it over, and the tractor started. Come to find out, there was lots of crankshaft end play, and this allowed the flywheel magnets to get too far away from the station-ary pole pieces. By pushing in a little on the crank, the magnets got a little closer, and it would start.

From that day forward, my Dad had no time for a Fordson tractor.

During World War II, tractors were almost impossible to find. There were few new ones being built, and for the duration, farmers had to get along with whatever they could find.

One of my relatives had a Massey-Harris Challenger, but renting some additional ground, he needed another tractor. After searching far and wide, the only thing he could find was a Minneapolis-Moline UDLX Comfortractor, the one with the enclosed cab, front bumper, and other accessories. A dealer had it on his lot for months, but no one would buy it . . . lots of farmers laughed about it, because, as they joked, "Only a sissy would run a tractor with a cab." Finally, he bought the tractor in desperation, and ran it during the war years.

With the coming of new tractors in 1946 and 1947, he gladly traded off the Comfortractor on a new Massey-Harris after the war. The ironic part of it was that he could hardly wait to get rid of the UDLX, and

Recollections

Generations of farmers and farm equipment come together in this painting by artist Walter Haskell Hinton for Deere & Company. (Deere & Company archives)

today it would probably be worth $15,000 to $20,000.

About twenty-five years ago, I made the acquaintance of an old fellow living about eighty rods off the road in what had once been a virtual showplace. This old guy was a bachelor, and once the old folks were gone, things fell into disrepair. I'll never forget that driveway all grown up in brush, with barely room enough for a car to drive through without rubbing on the brush. Once on the place, no less than twenty or twenty-five dogs arrived for a greeting—and they weren't friendly critters, either. The idea was to sit in the car and wait for the old fellow to come out of the house, and then the dogs all disappeared on command.

What led me to this place was the talk of some Moline Universal tractors and other equipment sitting around in an open-air shed, also called a blue-sky shed. The weeds had had their way for years, and I encountered the tallest horseweeds I've ever seen. Anyway, I asked the old gent about the tractors, and sure enough, there were four or five different Universals out in the weeds. Some were in pretty good shape; others were partially disassembled. To shorten a long story, we struck a deal, and I called some friends who went there in a few days to pick up the tractors as a lot, and they soon restored some of them. That was fortunate, because, subsequently, the old fellow died, and most everything else was junked.

One old-timer in the neighborhood had some of the poorest equipment around . . . most of it was somewhat beyond being worn out. Case threshing machines have a tubular return elevator, and we spent quite a lot of time repairing the chain when it broke—which was frequently. Getting the chain out of the tube and straightened out again was usually the biggest problem.

One time this fellow had to be gone for the day to a funeral, so my Dad and I were cutting oats. The tractor was a well-worn John Deere GP that hit on both cylinders some of the time. The grain binder was an old McCormick. A gib key on the back of the binder would come out every so often, and since there were never any spares of anything on hand, everyone was consigned to look in the stubble for the key that had come out. We looked for awhile and having no luck, started pawing through the toolbox.

In the box, there was an old screwdriver, a hammer, and a couple of mouse nests. Since we were about a half mile from the buildings, I suggested that we drive this old screwdriver into the keyway, and maybe that would hold until noon. We did, it held, and for several more years the old binder did its work with a screwdriver instead of a gib key.

John Deere tractors were very tolerant of poor maintenance, as attested to by the following incident:

When I was a youngster, we raised and sold registered Duroc hogs. We were to deliver a young boar to this fellow, and when we arrived, he was over in a little shed working on the old John Deere A. He was an affable fellow, and was telling us that he thought he should change the oil in the tractor, since it had been on the same oil all year. The oil was in five-gallon buckets, and why he didn't use the screw top, I'll never know. Instead, he pried off the lid and poured that way. I have no idea how long the lid had been off, but the chickens also enjoyed this little shed, and a coating of dust was plainly visible on top of the oil, along with a couple little feathers and other debris. Not to worry . . . the guy picked up the bucket—dirt, feathers, and all—and poured oil into the crankcase until it came out of the top petcock.

This same fellow also related how he had once cultivated corn and lost a shovel, but found it right away . . . stuck in the back tire!

Some folks took to engines and tractors with no problem at all. Others had little or no mechanical ability, and almost no understanding at all of farm power.

One old neighbor had, in his words, "a deuce of a time.'" For example, he had an old Monitor pump jack engine. The wind didn't blow, so there was hardly any water. This old fellow decided to hook up the engine to pump some water, but he had the spark too

"Henry"

FACING PAGE: *Henry Ford's Fordson is possibly the single most famous farm tractor ever made. Coming from a farm background in Dearborn, Michigan, Ford knew firsthand the toil of farming, and, in creating a lightweight and inexpensive tractor, he sought "To lift the burden of farming from flesh and blood and place it on steel and motors," as he wrote in his 1926 autobiography,* My Life and Work. *This 1926 Fordson Model F is owned by Fred Bissen. (Photograph by Andrew Morland)*

All in the family
A re-creation of the classic painting by artist Walter Haskell Hinton for Deere & Company, here featuring Allen Martin of Ephrata, Pennsylvania, alongside his 1939 Deere Model H. His grandsons, fourteen-year-old Glen Martin (center) and eight-year-old Mark Martin, sit in the driver's seat. (Photograph by Keith Baum)

much advanced, and when it kicked, somehow or other it dislocated his shoulder. Back in the 1940s, people didn't go to the hospital like today, and so they called the local doctor, who came driving out in a short time to see what he could do. He discovered the problem, and as the old guy laid there on the grass, doc kicked off his shoes, sat down with one foot in his armpit and the other against his neck. With a mighty heave he put the shoulder back in place, and the neighbor went about for the next couple of weeks with his arm in a sling.

There's a lesson here for everyone who cranks an engine or a tractor: Keep your thumb folded inside

your hand while cranking. If it kicks back, before you can release your thumb, it will cause your thumb some grievous injury, the crank will come back and break your arm, or in the case above, it will dislocate your shoulder.

During the winter months our old John Deere D stayed in the corn crib, belted to the Bear Cat hammermill. When done grinding, we slacked the belt until the next time. Usually, in real cold weather, we would fill the radiator with hot water to make it easier to start. However, we found that by using light oil and giving it a good prime of gasoline, the old D would usually start without this aid, even in the coldest weather. It was a good old tractor, and for many years was the biggest thing on the farm. About 1948 we converted it to rubber tires, and a couple years later, traded it off for a John Deere styled G.

This G was a good tractor, but caused all kinds of problems. Sometimes it would throw a fit after it was hot, and it wouldn't run very well at all. After eventually replacing the magneto, it ran just fine. In 1951, it left the premises, being traded in on a new Massey-Harris 44 tractor.

In our neighborhood, there was a fellow who had been a longtime thresherman. He had two Aultman-Taylor 30/60 tractors and a 25/50 Aultman-Taylor. In the neighborhood, the 30/60 was called the mud turtle, because farmers claimed that a mud turtle would move faster than the old 30/60 when threshing.

About 1950, this old fellow offered the three tractors to my Dad for $150—that was for all three! We were still threshing, and continued to do so until 1958. I earnestly implored my Dad to buy them, but he didn't. I sure wish those three tractors were still setting there along the fenceline as I remember them!

As a kid, it was fun listening to the old-timers relating their escapades and recalling the various kinds of tractors in the neighborhood. One of the popular ones was the IHC Titan 10/20; we had lots of these. There were a few Bull tractors, and a few Heider tractors—the latter was highly regarded in the area. Waterloo Boy and Hart-Parr were popular, since both were built within a hundred miles of our neighborhood. Another popular model was the Moline Universal, along with a few Rumely OilPull tractors. Aultman-Taylor tractors seemed to be more predominant than the OilPull in our area; the county had several Aultman-Taylor tractors for road work, and several threshing rings used them. We had a few Fordson tractors in our neighborhood, but they were not as popular as the IHC Titan. By the 1930s, the Oliver became popular, as was the John Deere row-crop design. In rank order, the most popular of 1940 was probably the Deere, followed by the Farmall, then Oliver, followed by Case, Allis-Chalmers, and a few others. There was a Minneapolis-Moline dealership in the area, and a fair number of these models were also around the neighborhood. I recall a single Silver King, and one copy of the B. F. Avery Model V tractor.

In 1952, our neighbor bought a nearly new Caterpillar D-6 bulldozer. Words can hardly describe my fascination as I watched this outfit dig out trees and do many other jobs. When it was close by, the sound of that six-cylinder engine was like music. After my neighbor had used it for some thirty years, he passed away. Now I have that same old D-6, and still enjoy listening to that beautiful stack music. The engine now has over 18,000 hours, and in all those years it had a valve job once. Other than that, it's the same as when it came from the factory.

On my dad's side of the family, they were all blacksmiths, threshermen, and well drillers, except for my grandfather, who farmed. My Uncle Jake was a crackerjack blacksmith who died young in the 1918 influenza epidemic. As a kid, I was told the following story at different times by several old-timers, related from when they were kids:

Uncle Jake had a blacksmith shop, and one day a fellow came into his shop with a 1½ hp engine of some make or other in the back of his wagon. The engine was badly busted up: This resulted from one day when it wouldn't start, and so the fellow took a hammer or something to it and vented his wrath. After that, it for sure wouldn't run. Soon, his anger abated, so he brought it in to be repaired.

Eventually Uncle Jake got word to this fellow to come pick up his engine. He came, and asked for the bill, to which he got the answer of $20. Bear in mind that in those days a new 1½ hp engine could be bought for $40 or so. The fellow had somewhat of a temper we're told, and demanded to know why the bill was so high. Uncle Jake replied, "$10 for fixing the engine, and $10 for busting it up . . . either pay it or I'll take it out of your hide!" He paid, they loaded up the engine, and that's the story.

I used to hear the story, too, about how some old-timer couldn't get his car started in the winter, so he went to a druggist, got some ether, and proceeded to pour some in each cylinder. He then cranked the engine, this stuff lit off, and literally stripped the cylinder head off the studs, completely wrecking the engine.

My fascination with old engines and tractors began

Case tractors, then . . .

LEFT: *J. I. Case once lead the field with its steam traction engines, but the company was not quick to produce gas-powered tractors, even though it experimented with prototypes early on. This 1941 Case SC-3 was Case's two-plow general-purpose model; here it pulls a Case Model A baler. (Photograph by J. C. Allen and Son)*

at about the age of eight. Christmas Day was always spent at my maternal grandparents; my grandpa had been a steam engineer in earlier years. While digging in their storeroom, I came across the famous book, *Farm Engines and How to Run Them*. After begging it off of my grandparents, I took it home and virtually memorized it from cover to cover. That was the beginning of my fascination for old engines and tractors.

Back in the late 1960s, a group of us were displaying engines at the Midwest Old Threshers Reunion at Mt. Pleasant, Iowa. Somehow the conversation turned to engine builders in Iowa, particularly those in Waterloo. The idea was offered that someone should dig out this information and put it together. As a result, I published the book, *History of Gas Engine & Tractor Builders in Iowa*, in 1971.

Subsequently, I did some other books, and had the good fortune to be "discovered" by George Dammann of Crestline Publishing in 1976. That led to my first full-length book, *Encyclopedia of American Farm Tractors* in 1979. Since that time, I've written about thirty books, and since 1985, I've written a monthly "Reflections" column in *Gas Engine Magazine*. My latest title, *Encyclopedia of American Farm Implements* is being published by Krause Publications. It is the first comprehensive pictorial history to be published on the development of farm implements and machinery.

If someone had told me thirty years ago that I'd end up writing books on old engines and tractors, I'd have thought them daft. Occasionally, people ask me how to do a big book and keep all the facts and figures together. That's hard to explain . . . over thirty years of it have made me develop my own special methods of doing things. I suppose that if I was to take on a partner at this point in my life, he or she would probably throw up his or her hands in despair after a couple of hours.

I think it's a shame that there never has been a gas engine on a postage stamp, because there's no part of today's life that isn't somehow affected by the gas engine.

. . . Case tractors, now

ABOVE: *A 1946 Case DC wide front. This tractor was restored by the Escalon, California, Future Farmers of America. Owner: University of California at Davis. (Photograph by Ralph W. Sanders)*

Driving tractor, then . . .

RIGHT: *While the men go off to fight in World War II, this woman takes over the Deere in this painting by artist Walter Haskell Hinton for Deere & Company. (Deere & Company archives)*

. . . Driving tractor, now

BELOW: *While her father harvests rocks, Darla Zietz takes a common childhood chore on the farm, piloting the family's tractor. The Mennonite family's farm is near Churchtown, Pennsylvania. (Photograph by Jerry Irwin)*

Starting young, then . . .

LEFT: *A timeless scene from the local "machinery hill" at state and county fairs everywhere: A youngster tries out the steering on a monstrous Minneapolis-Moline GB Diesel at the Minnesota State Fair in the 1950s. (Minnesota State Fair collection)*

. . . Starting young, now

BELOW: *Another timeless scene from today's threshing bees and tractor meets everywhere: Three Amish children follow their father, as they examine a lineup of steam traction engines at the Rough and Tumble Thresherman's Reunion in Lancaster County, Pennsylvania. (Photograph by Jerry Irwin)*

THE JT TRACTOR
By Norman Pripps of Wisconsin, 1919

When I was nine years old, my father shopped for a crawler tractor for sled-hauling logs to his sawmill in northern Wisconsin. Tractors from Holt had a good reputation, but were too large for the job he had in mind. The new Cletrac was too small. Advertisements by the JT Tractor Company of Cleveland, Ohio, indicated their 16/30 model, about 3½ tons in weight, would be just right. By mail, Dad ordered one, giving directions for shipping.

About a month later, the new JT arrived on its own flat car, pushed out to Hemlock Camp on the logging spur along with log-hauling cars. Dad was a steam engine man, and did not much care for these newfangled contraptions, so he told my older brother, Ray, then sixteen, to figure out how to start it and drive it. He had done the same thing with a new Model T Ford bought two years earlier; he told my older brother, "You drive it, you fix it."

We got along with the JT just fine, hauling two sleds of logs at a time. We found that it wouldn't run well on kerosene in the cold weather, so we always ran it on gasoline. The only trouble we had was that we broke one of the frame rails. Dad got a ¾-inch piece of steel to act as a doubler for the broken frame rail. We had to hand-drill ½-inch bolt holes to attach this reinforcement. That took several days.

One spring, my brother Ray and the JT broke through the ice road and fell into a sink hole. After one or two efforts to get out, the JT had sunk in to the top of the tracks and was gradually going down. Dad quickly bolted steel plates to track links on each side, hooked chains to holes in the plates, then hooked the chains around trees on the far side of the sink hole. With a mighty snort, the JT hoisted itself up and out of the sink hole, and we all heaved sighs of relief.

Deere tractors, then . . .

FACING PAGE: *A trio of salesmen show off their wares: the new styled Deere Model A with the Roll-O-Matic front end. This display was set up at the Minnesota State Fair in the 1940s, but looks much the same today, although it now features the latest in tractor models and hat styles. (Minnesota State Fair collection)*

. . . Deere tractors, now

ABOVE: *A beautifully restored unstyled 1934 Deere Model A. Owner: Bill Ruffner of Bellevue, Nebraska. (Photograph by Ralph W. Sanders)*

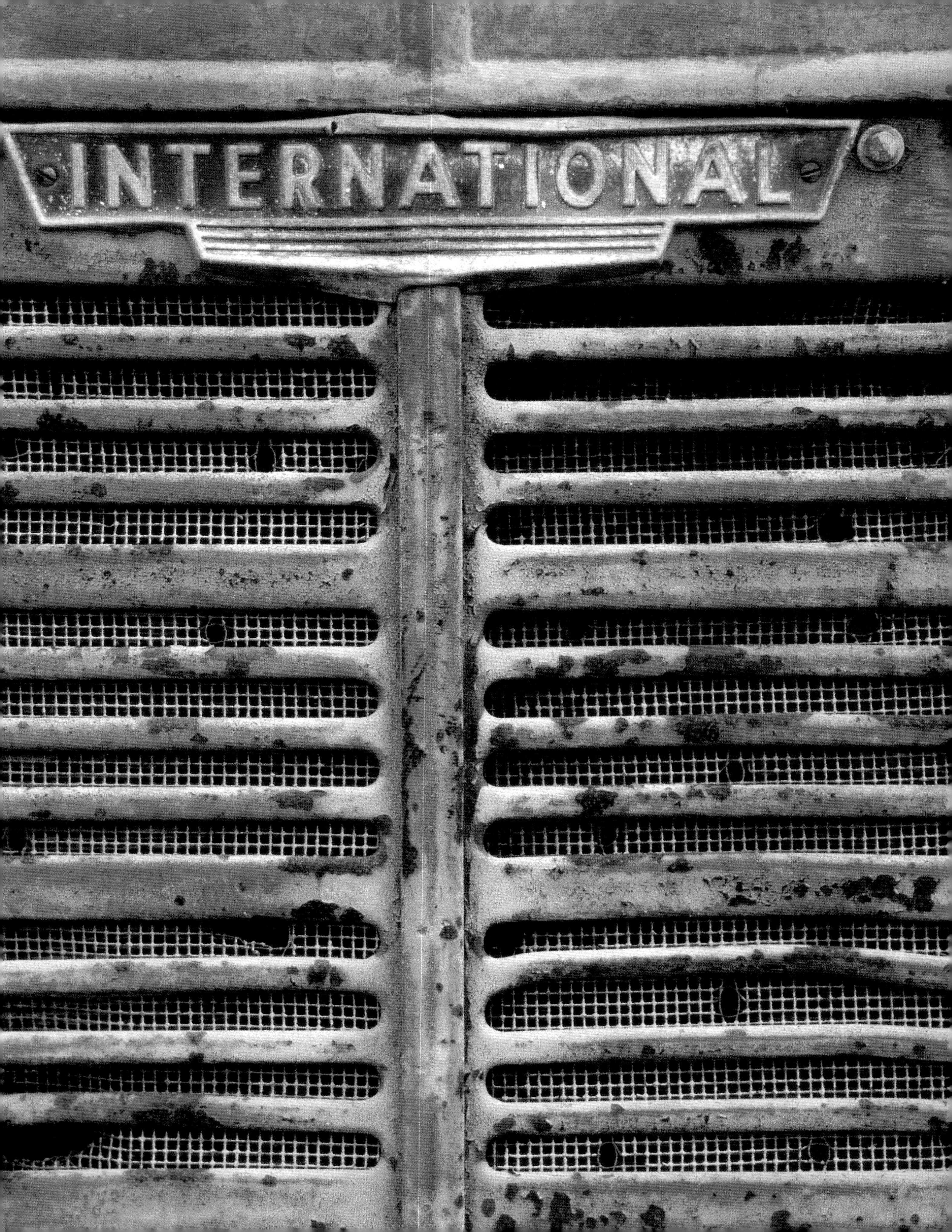
INTERNATIONAL

Subterfuge

By Patricia Penton Leimbach

Patricia Penton Leimbach is farming's Erma Bombeck. Like Bombeck, author of numerous essays and books on being a housewife, Leimbach is a sage philosopher on the trials and tribulations of everyday life. She writes with a sharp pen about the joys and troubles, the hard work and humor, the meaning and value of rural living.

Leimbach was raised on a fruit farm near Lorain, Ohio. Alongside her husband Paul, a fourth-generation farmer, she has run End o' Way farm in Vermilion, Ohio, just a few miles from her childhood home, for more than four decades. But it is through her writing that Leimbach has become one of the best-known farm women in North America. For many years, she authored the weekly "Country Wife" column in the Elyria (Ohio) *Chronicle Telegram.* Leimbach also has three books to her credit, *A Thread of Blue Denim, All My Meadows,* and *Harvest of Bittersweet,* all filled with wit and wisdom culled from her firsthand farming knowledge, concerning everything from raising puppies to driving farm tractors.

In this essay from *Harvest of Bittersweet,* she describes the brilliant subterfuge used by her husband to get her to agree that it is time for yet another new tractor on the farm.

You can "smell" a new tractor coming two or three years ahead. The first thing a wife notices is that the thrill—of the old tractor, that is—is gone. He no longer fondles the fenders, caresses the hood. No more does he run in the face of a storm to get 'er under cover. A crumpled muffle may leap into the wind for months on end. The vinyl seat splits and he seems not to notice. Foam oozes from the rupture and is carelessly obscured beneath a feed bag. Gone is the pride that once moved him to slyly detour visitors through the tractor shed. It doesn't seem very important anymore who drives the old thing—the wife even gets a crack at it.

"Give you any trouble?" he'll ask casually at lunch. Then, as he chomps down on a cob of corn, he'll move into phase two of the buildup: innuendo and suggestion.

"Been startin' a little hard lately. Thought maybe you'd notice. . . . Shifts a little rough, don't you think?" You can agree or disagree. The psychological workup is in progress. The seeds of disturbances have been sown.

"D'ja notice how much oil that tractor's been burning?" he'll say to his son one day, making sure you're within earshot. Then early some morning he'll interrupt the bookkeeping by walking into the kitchen (ostensibly for something to eat) and remarking, "Guess how much we spent for repairs on the 706 last year?" And then he'll name a figure half again as high as the household budget.

"What?" you shriek. "On that new tractor?"

"That new tractor is ten years old."

"You're kidding."

Time for a new tractor
The worn, bruised, and rusted grille of an International tractor. (Photograph by Vincent Manocchi)

Farm family and tractor, then . . .

Farmer Harry Wood and family of Yellow Jacket, Colorado, stand proudly in front of their family tractor. This Minneapolis-Moline UDLX Comfortractor was the first sold in 1938 by the Midwestern division of Minne-Mo's marketing organization, according to the original company archive photograph. The UDLX was the first farm tractor with an enclosed cab, and with its special gearing, M-M marketed it as a tractor for the whole family. It could plow fields during the week and then be driven to church on Sunday. (Minnesota Historical Society collection)

"I am not kidding. We bought it the year the willow tree fell on the outhouse. Remember? I'll tell you how long we've had that tractor. We've had it so long it's paid for."

The next thing you know, there's a tractor dealer coming by on trumped-up charges, hanging around the gas pump, leaving slick, four-color brochures in your kitchen, "giving" your husband the kind of time he's charging $10 an hour for back at the shop.

Someplace in the campaign you'll be treated to the "poor lil' ol' me" routine.

"Russ and Chuck traded their John Deeres in on a coupl'a 4-wheel-drive Cases two years ago. Don, Lenny, George, and Bob—they've all had a complete tractor turnover since we bought that 706. . . ."

Then there's the scare technique: "Parts are gettin' harder and harder to locate for that machine.

Wouldn't surprise me a bit if they quit making them altogether."

About this time you'll find a list of figures on a scratch pad conveniently placed to catch your eye—over the sink next to the telephone, on the back of the john. You think at first it's an inventory of all your holdings.

"Is this anything you want to keep?" you ask.

"Oh, that—that's just something the tractor dealer jotted down for me. Uhhh . . . some figures on a tractor—and a plow. New tractor takes a new plow. Says he'll take my old tractor on trade and give me just what I paid for it ten years ago. That takes 'er down to about fourteen thousand."

"Fourteen thousand dollars! Holy cow! We don't want to buy the business. We just need a tractor!"

You suddenly realize that it's all over.

... Farm family and tractor, now

Farmer John Martin and family of Churchtown, Pennsylvania, pose proudly with their Case tractor in the 1990s. (Photograph by Keith Baum)

Father and son at the wheel

A father-and-son team share the steering wheel of their Canadian Massey-Harris in the Parade of Power at the Rough and Tumble Thresherman's Reunion in Lancaster County, Pennsylvania. Massey-Harris had a long, involved, complicated history of mergers, takeovers, and contract-built tractors. It all began in 1891 when Daniel Massey's Massey Manufacturing Company of Toronto, Ontario, joined with Alanson Harris's A. Harris, Son & Company of Brantford, Ontario. The firm, now called Massey-Ferguson and headquartered in Toronto, is still going strong. (Photograph by Jerry Irwin)

WOMAN'S INFLUENCE IN TRACTOR BUYING
Investigation by *The Farmer*, 1919

The manufacturer or the distributor who may seldom come into actual contact with the tractor buyer usually thinks of the farmer or his son as the only persons of importance to be convinced in the sale of tractors. The salesman in the field who is actually getting signatures to tractor sales contracts knows that there is another influence, just as powerful, and just as much to be recognized, as the influence of the farmer and his sons. That influence is the farm woman. Local tractor salesmen who have recognized and given consideration to the farm woman have been amply repaid for doing so.... [T]here is ... a preponderance of evidence to show that the woman's influence must be considered, and her favorable opinion won to the use of the tractor if tractor sales are to reach their maximum possibilities.

Two hundred and seventy-seven farmers who do not own tractors have reported as to their wives' attitudes, and these reports contain very strong evidence that the women in many cases are responsible for their husbands not owning tractors. Forty-six and one-half per cent of the total number of farmers reporting state that their wives are unfavorable to the purchase of tractors. It is most evident from these reports that it would not be necessary to sell the woman in regard to the individual make of tractor to be bought, but that it is necessary to sell her on the power farming idea,

especially as it applies to tractors, before any progress in the sale of a tractor to her husband could be made.

The farm woman sees possible objections to tractors which her husband does not see. Many of them object to tractors because the tractor means more greasy clothes in the family washing, more days away from home if her husband does custom work. These and other items which men might not think of are of vital importance to the farm woman.

On the other hand, many farm women appreciate the advantages of tractors, and see in them advantages which the salesman or manufacturer might not realize were there. If the tractor displaces horses, it also makes unnecessary to that extent evening and morning chores. If the tractor decreases farm drudgery, it helps keep the boys at home. If the tractor can operate all day in the blistering heat without fatigue, it saves the horses, which appeals to the humane instincts of the farm woman. If it decreases the number of farm hands, it decreases, correspondingly, the farm woman's work, and, finally, if it increases farm profits, it increases for her and her children the opportunities for happiness.

Apparently, therefore, it is vital to the tractor industry that farm women be sold on power farming, and this is a point which every manufacturer and advertising manager may well consider carefully.

Family farm, family tractor

Herb Garber, left, leans against his faithful Allis-Chalmers with his brother Gene at right. Their father, Henry, sits in the saddle. They farm near Elizabethtown, Pennsylvania. (Photograph by Jerry Irwin)

Everything the farm family needed, 1930s

LEFT: A *Minneapolis-Moline advertising photograph from the company archives showing all of the equipment needed for a family farm in the 1930s— all of it being from Minne-Mo, naturally. This M-M–only farm was owned by Joe Kudiac of Hennessey, Oklahoma.* (Minnesota Historical Society collection)

Everything the farm family needed, 1960s

ABOVE: A *farm magazine photograph showing all of the equipment needed for a family farm in the 1960s, including a mix of Deere and Minneapolis-Moline equipment.* (Photograph by J. C. Allen and Son)

Minneapolis-Moline tractors, then . . .
ABOVE: *Minneapolis-Moline dealers meet in the 1930s under the shade of a tree in Columbus, Ohio, to examine the latest Prairie Gold offering. (Minnesota Historical Society collection)*

. . . Minneapolis-Moline tractors, now
LEFT: *A Minneapolis-Moline Model Z workhorse at the Antique Gas & Steam Engine Museum at Vista, California. (Photograph by Vincent Manocchi)*

FARMALL CUB MYSTERY
By Duane Carden of Wisconsin, 1950

Grampa got a new little Farmall Cub, using it to pull a fairly large binder, which it handled remarkably well. We would unhook the binder in the field and drive the Cub home for lunch. We kids used to pick the Cub up and turn it around 180 degrees, putting it back in its tracks, but facing the other way. We did this quite a few times before Grampa caught on.

RAMBLINGS AT THE THRESHERMEN'S REUNION
By Ed Klimuska of Lancaster County, Pennsylvania

David Cox lives on a farm in Rising Sun, Maryland. He works as a golf course mechanic for a living. Along with his father, Earl, David collects International Harvester Farmall tractors. He has a 1929 model Farmall tractor that has steel wheels. It's a favorite.

"Buying old tractors and restoring them is something we have fun with," he says. "I like to tinker. He likes the old stuff. I do all the mechanical work. He supplies the resources. It's a hobby and we have fun. We've been playing with tractors for quite a while. It keeps us out of trouble.

"At first, they weren't too expensive. Now, they're getting expensive."

Like grandfather, like grandson
Allen Martin of Ephrata, Pennsylvania, sits on his 1935 Deere Model B, while his grandson, three-year-old Jonathan Martin, pilots a Model 60 pedal tractor. (Photograph by Keith Baum)

Chapter 3

Threshing Days

*"A good steam engineer should be sober, industrious,
careful, and faithful to his charge."*
—J. I. Case's *Young Engineer's Guide* steam engine instruction book

Threshing day was a social event on the farm like no other. Neighboring farm families gathered to share the burden of work and a good meal—and ultimately, to share the rewards, as the cooperation on threshing day ensured that each family reaped the harvest.

These stories of a time gone by tell of threshing days using steam power, as well as gasoline tractors, to drive the belt of the threshers before the coming of the combine.

🌾

Threshing days continue
LARGE PHOTO: *A threshing scene from the 1990s on an Old Order Amish farm in Lancaster County, Pennsylvania. (Photograph by Jerry Irwin)*

Threshing days of yore
INSET: *A 1912 Case 20/40 gas and kerosene tractor powers a thresher in the 1910s. (Peter Letourneau collection)*

Threshing Day

By A. C. Wood

Canadian farmer and folk philosopher A. C. Wood wrote eloquently of rural life on the Canadian prairies in his colorful tome, *Old Days on the Farm*, from 1918. He tells of great farming events in those pioneering years, from old-timers's homesteading yarns to the day when the circus came to a nearby town. His book is a valuable first-person history, a collection of farming lore and personal insight of another era told by someone who lived through the years in which agriculture underwent the dramatic change of mechanization.

In this excerpt, he recalls the hard work and great joys that were the threshing days, remembering the different eras of threshing, from flailing with a "poverty stick" to the early horse-driven powers to the arrival of the steam traction engine.

Most every one who knows anything of country life has some knowledge of a "threshing day" on the farm—that's the occasion when with the assistance of his neighbours, a farmer has his grain separated from the chaff and straw incident to its growth. In the good old days, long before the modern steam threshing outfit was thought of, the flail, or, as it was sometimes termed, "the poverty stick" was in general use.

When I was a boy there were several flails about our barn, although the horse-power and separator were then in evidence. Peas were usually flailed out and sometimes tramped or treaded out with oxen or horses on the ground just as in Biblical times the husbandmen separated the corn from the straw and chaff. It was held by some old-time farmers that peas were too much split or broken, by the threshing machine, and that the straw was reduced almost to cut feed and dust. Most farmers kept sheep then and clean pea-straw was looked on as a favourite food for the wool producers.

Peas were harvested in those days with scythes and were usually cut a little on the green side of maturity and the straw made excellent fodder. Consequently, most farmers flailed out the pea crop and winter was the season for such work. The operation would be conducted on the barn floor and it was quite a sight to watch two or three sturdy men start in on a bed of peas and with rhythmic motion of their bodies and with beat as steady and regular as army drummers, pound and pound away till the peas would all be loosened from the pods and on the floor below the straw.

I do not recall that the flailers had songs or chanteys for such occasion, as sailors have, while reeling at the capstan of a ship, but such they might well have had. It would have made the toil easier and assisted the toilers in keeping time.

As a boy I considered myself quite an artist with the "poverty stick," and I remember that I attained efficiency only after I had dented my head in various places. It may be explained that the flail was formed

Threshing day

Powered by an Eclipse steam traction engine from the Frick Company of Waynesboro, Pennsylvania, threshing days continue on this Old Order Amish farm in Lancaster County, Pennsylvania. (Photograph by Jerry Irwin)

of two pieces of wood—hickory wood was the most favoured—the handle would be, perhaps, two feet longer than the wooden lash which was joined to it with a swivel, this latter cunningly made by hand. Unless one exercised some care it was quite within the realm of possibility to acquire a self-inflicted bump on the head. Of course, a skilled operator, using this old-time threshing instrument, would be immune but a greenhorn would be running in great luck if he escaped some hard knocks in the schooling of flailing experience.

Many farmers, too, used to thresh oats for feed, in the early fall, with the flail. Machine threshing, in those days, was done much later in the season than in these modern times. As horses were necessary for power and there was the ploughing to be done, threshing was put off till the fall work was well along and cool weather had set in. In order to get oats for horse feed, many farmers would flail sheaves, partly, without untying them, and put these through the machine to complete the job, when it arrived.

That's how I learned the art of hitting something else than my head, with a flail. I recall that I had dreams of beating a big drum some day but the fates intervened.

"Threshing Day," with the machine, was, of course, of more than ordinary interest to the farmer and his household. Dairying was not then so extensively engaged in, the grain crop being of premier importance. The neighbours would be there to assist and several would bring their teams along for use on the horse-power. I presume, even most folks, in this day, would know a horse-power at sight. It was a combination of one great cogged, metal wheel and several smaller ones and had wooden arms extending from the centre to which the horses were attached. The teams went around in a circle and the driver, with a whip of wood and buckskin, stood on a small platform in the centre of the merry-go-round affair. It was quite a science to keep five teams pulling steadily and if this were not effected, the result would be varying speed in the threshing machine and that meant poorly threshed grain. A trained driver could tell by the roar of the machinery if the proper speed was being maintained and so cracked his whip accordingly.

In those days a barn would usually be packed to the roof as there was little or no early threshing and there would often be a stack of grain behind the barn

as well—an overflow, as it were, that could not be stored inside. It was often a two-day job to thresh out a farmer's crop. The machines in use then were smaller and the power limited to the dynamic energy ten horses could supply.

I recall that, as a small boy, I was lifted up by a thresherman that I might gaze into the greedy maw that contained the buzzing cylinder of the machine. On that separator's side was painted its name—"The Roaring Lion"—and my first look into it convinced me that it had been properly named, and I feared it just as much as if it had actually been a King of Beasts.

I remember the strawstack was the place of chief interest for a small boy. There were, of course, no pneumatic tubes to put the straw where it was wanted, on the old-time machine, but there were straw-carriers, a sort of elevator, and there would usually be half a dozen men on the stack. These old-time strawstacks were sometimes enormous mounds of straw, built in pyramid form, and often higher than the barn roof.

I have in mind recollections of a favourite trick that the boys of the neighbourhood used frequently to play in connection with "threshing day" and the strawstack. While the men would be at dinner, the boys would dig a hole on top of the rather loosely-built strawstacks, to the depth of five or six feet, or as deep as time and juvenile energy would permit. They'd cover the hole over lightly with straw, and set the pitchforks of the men in such a position that they'd have to walk across the pit to reach their tools. The young scamps would hide about and wait for events to shape themselves and when some old chap, on returning to work, would fall into the hole and, as it were, pull the hole in after him, in the shape of a big heap of loose straw, the joy of the boys would be full and complete. You see a fall of a few feet into loose straw was not likely to hurt any one, the trick, therefore, was not frowned upon and it added greatly to juvenile happiness.

The old strawstack made a great playhouse for children. They'd dig caves and grottoes into it and slide down its sloping sides like an alpine climber making a descent across a snow-field.

The day's threshing over, I recall that the men lingered after supper and often a social evening would be spent at the farmhouse. Some of the young women of the neighbourhood who had been assisting in feed-

Sunrise
Threshing day always started at first light, and often ran from "can" to "can't"—from when you can see as the sun rises, to when you can't see as the sun sets. (Photograph by Jerry Irwin)

THRESHING MEALS
By Ruth Barstow of Peoria, Illinois

This gal down the road south of here . . . was so high-falutin' and bragging on her threshing dinners all the time. She'd say that her meals were *always* eaten up, you know that the men were *always* eating up everything she put out. And, my gosh, we always felt like it was better to have food left over. If they ate everything, why how could she be sure they'd had enough to eat.

ing the "hungry horde" would be there. There would be games—perhaps, an impromptu dance when the boys would shake all the chaff out of their hair. "Old Zip Coon" and other classics would be butchered on the fiddle or there might be a quiet game of euchre if the old folks had not too great a horror of "the devil's pasteboards." To-day, I am informed, all the men hurry home after supper and that the modern threshing is not the social event it once was and it is to be regretted that it is so.

Dear reader, have you ever been stationed at the head of the straw-carriers at an old-time threshing, when the dust was so thick, as the saying is, that it could be cut with a knife? On a stack where there was plenty of air such a position was not too bad, but with the carriers running up into a barn mow, and almost against the roof, the man at the head of the straw elevator, occupied a tough, tough place.

I recall, when I was a lad, along with another youth, I was so placed. Room was scarce and the grain was heavy fall wheat. Early in the afternoon we had shouted down to the man who was feeding the hungry monster to hurry along—that we just couldn't keep from freezing for want of something to do. Just joking, we were, of course. When there was scarcely room to work, for the straw filled up behind us, he threw sheaves into that cylinder at a most remarkable rate. We were getting well winded but it wouldn't do to let the straw pile up at the elevator head as it would stop the machine, and would also be an acknowledgment that we were "all in." We were both young, dust-covered, thirsty, sweaty and exhausted. "I'll make those two young rascals cry 'Help' or 'Enough,'" the feeder, no doubt, was saying to himself. I may explain that the elevator was run by a long chain from the machine to a pulley at the top and as it was getting dusk, and he couldn't be seen doing it, my partner in distress threw the chain off the pulley and saved the situation. This chain occasionally jumped off of its own accord and so we were not suspected. It gave us a much needed breathing spell, also an opportunity to get the straw well back from our position and so we held the fort without a surrender. If that patriotic song "We'll Never Let the Old Flag Fall," had been extant then I guess we'd both have been singing it as we worked.

I remember an open cylinder machine was used in our district to thresh peas. The grain was forked

Portrait of a threshing day

The threshing crew—including the womenfolk and children out for a visit—pause to pose for the photographer in Walsh County, North Dakota, in the 1890s. (Minnesota Historical Society collection)

Threshing crew, then . . .

ABOVE: *The E. A. Jones threshing outfit posed for a studio photograph in Martin County, Minnesota, circa 1890. (Minnesota Historical Society collection)*

. . . Threshing crew, now

LEFT: *Obviously a veteran of more than one threshing bee and tractor meet, John Wall feeds coal into a steam traction engine at the Rough and Tumble Thresherman's Reunion in Lancaster County, Pennsylvania, in the 1990s. (Photograph by Jerry Irwin)*

into the cylinder and straw and grain went out together to the ground behind. By some means a stone hidden in the straw was thrown in and a shower of broken granite and steel teeth from the cylinder flew into the air. The two young fellows forking in the grain faded away from the vicinity in haste, and no wonder. But the old chap who owned the outfit had this to say to them, "Ye'd make mighty poor sodjers, you two, if ye'd run from the likes o' that."

But the flail has gone forever and the horsepower, at least as a means of threshing, is almost a curiosity. Has the acme of efficiency been reached in the modern steam traction engine and self-feeding and stack-building separator? Who knows?

In my homesteading days in the Northwest I saw power for threshing operated with oxen, but the teams moved too slowly and had to be rested often. The driver told me the animals got dizzy going around in a circle, and, to get best results, the critters should be unhitched frequently and turned about in the opposite direction to take the twists out of them. Of course, he was just stringing me.

During one of the "lean" years in the West, in the early eighties, many of us far Western homesteaders had difficulty in keeping the wolf from the door, indeed, some of us held that the wolves were in packs. Along with others of my neighbours I journeyed down into Manitoba and joined a threshing outfit. Wages were small but we needed the money real badly, consequently we put pride and the agricultural independence engendered within us by the ownership of prairie homesteads, behind us, and "hired out."

The party to which I was attached went threshing on the plains about Portage La Prairie, then one of the most prosperous farm settlements in the West. For four weeks we threshed in the fields and for many weeks longer from the stacks. Not a drop of rain fell in all that time. It was an ideal season for saving the Western crop. We had an ox-team and a horse-team with us—the former hauled the engine, brought water in a tank and pulled the straw away from the rear of the machine with a long rope—the horses drew the separator about from place to place. We were boarded by the farmers but carried our bedding with us and slept in granaries, stables and sheds. Most farmhouses in those days were very small and the advent of sixteen men meant crowding. Those who were crowded out went to the stable or granary. To-day, I am informed, many Western outfits—and there are thousands in the West now—have their own cabooses to sleep in and furnish their own meals.

Compared with the "Threshing Day" meals that I remember in Old Ontario, that Western grub was poor indeed. Down here at least, the women of the farmer's household vied with each other in old days, in furnishing the most appetising and attractive meals that could be produced. Out West we had potatoes, bread, glucose syrup, salt pork and a very indifferent quality of butter. Fruit was a luxury, indeed, and rarely on the bill-of-fare in any form. But we had appetites, oh, my!

I recall one evening that our outfit was domiciled in a bachelor's small frame house near Lake Manitoba. The whole sixteen were sleeping in the loft on the floor when a "surprise party" of young folks from High Bluff or Poplar Point, invaded that bachelor's home. They had driven nearly twenty miles across the prairie to "surprise" him and it was a surprise, indeed. They didn't know he had a threshing outfit on his hands. There were fiddlers, lunch baskets and girls with the invaders and our noble sixteen stole into their clothing in haste and joined in the jubilation. We made a night of it. There was, likely, chaff in our hair, and I know there were no frills on our clothing. I know, too, that there was no chaff left on us after that dance. We shook it all off in our efforts to see which of us could hit the lumber hardest with our leathers. All the dances had corners on them and the fiddler "chawed " tobacco. The old boy who "called off" the dances was our ox-driver and he'd yell out instructions as if he were guiding his horned critters. As a social function in the "wild and woolly," it might properly have been termed "an enjoyable occasion."

Mapping the Farm

By John Hildebrand

John Hildebrand's book, *Mapping the Farm: The Chronicle of a Family*, is an elegy to four generations of farmers that built a life on the land near Rochester, Minnesota. The story starts in the 1880s, when William O'Neill began raising dairy cows, and continues for one hundred years to the day when William's grandson, Ed, is getting too old to farm and must face the future.

This excerpt tells of the arrival of farm power, beginning on the day when William's son, John, is waiting at the railroad depot for the steam traction engine he has ordered. The new machine brings a change to the family's life, broadening their goals and their horizons.

John is also the author of *Reading the River: A Voyage Down the Yukon*. He lives in Eau Claire, Wisconsin, and teaches at the University of Wisconsin.

On April 22, 1991, John rode to the railroad depot in Simpson to take delivery of the Reeves twenty-horsepower steam traction engine he had ordered the month before from an implement company in Minneapolis. The tractor was as big as a locomotive and burned a ton of coal a day. He had taken out a chattel mortgage for $2,215 to buy it and go into the threshing business.

When the tractor was unloaded from its flatcar, Berne St. George stoked the firebox until he had a head of steam. Then John eased the clutch lever out and the tractor pulled away from the depot, chugging down the road at four miles an hour. The two men rode high above the roadbed on a platform behind the boiler, sheltered from falling sparks by a black sunroof. Behind them they towed a rattling wooden tank wagon. The Reeves' five-foot lug wheels gave the passengers an elevated view of the country-side. John steered with one hand on the wheel and the other on the throttle lever, keeping constant watch on the steam gauge. Boiler explosions involving steam tractors averaged two a day across the country—newspaper accounts always made a point of reporting the distance victims were thrown—but the biggest danger, due to the machine's great weight, was a bridge collapse, so drivers preferred fording creeks to crossing unfamiliar bridges. But there were no bridges between Simpson and the farm. When the Reeves chugged down the last grade and turned into the yard, scattering chickens, John tooted the shiny brass whistle and Mame and the children watched from the porch as the steam engine hissed to a stop in front of them.

Steam tractors were too slow and ponderous to replace horses at most field work, except for pulling stumps or plowing unbroken sod. When the eight-bottom gang plow John bought to pull behind the Reeves proved too heavy (a man riding on a platform above the plow had to raise and lower the shares),

Steam power

Wood-and-steel Northwest steam traction engines of monstrous proportions parade down the street of Stillwater, Minnesota, from the Northwest Thresher Company factory in 1909. Northwest's gas tractors and threshers were relabeled by the American-Abell Engine & Threshing Company in Toronto, Ontario, and widely sold in the Canadian market. Another version of Northwest's gas Universal was built and sold by the Hero Manufacturing Company of Winnipeg, Manitoba, in the 1910s. Northwest was bought out by Rumely in 1912. (Minnesota Historical Society collection)

he gave it to the St. George brothers, who took it out to the Dakotas, where a farmer could plow a straight line into the next county. Essentially, the steam tractor was a portable power source for running other machinery such as a sawmill or a separator. John bought the Reeves to start his own threshing ring, which, like the nursery stock business, was a way of making money off the farm. Threshing began in late July and extended into October. The order of farms alternated, but there was always an urgency to the run because once the grain was cut a stretch of bad weather could ruin it. Now that he owned the tractor and separator, the threshing run would begin at home.

Early morning. The sky was pale and cloudless except for a smudge of black smoke rising above an oat field over east. The oats had been cut and bundled the week before, the bundles stacked in shocks and lined up in neat rows to dry. Now a dozen wagons slowly drove down the rows. At each shock the driver stopped, wrapped the reins around the wagon post, and began to build a load of bundles on the rack. Two blasts of a steam whistle signaled that the separator was working, and all over the field men and horses quickened their pace, all of them inextricably connected to a whirring machine whose appetite for grain never slackened. When the rack reached his own height, the wagon driver flicked his reins and his team cropped across the stubble field toward a black cloud funneling from the Reeves' smokestack.

The steam tractor stood hissing in the center of the field. Across from it was a canary-yellow Avery separator, a narrow, shivering contraption of sheet metal and wood with a long-necked spout at one end that shot a constant stream of straw and chaff into the air. The two machines were connected by seventy-five feet of whirring canvas belt that snaked between them like voltage leaping a gap. Wagons lined up along either side of the separator as drivers waited their turn to pitch bundles into the machine before heading back to the field for another load. Most teams were used to the noise and heat of the boiler, but even with blinders a new horse might shy if it caught sight of the belt streaking past or sniffed the unfamiliar tang of coal smoke and hot grease.

Berne St. George sat on the platform beside the firebox, chain-smoking and keeping one eye on the pressure gauge. If the needle fell below forty, he'd swing the fire door open, exposing his shins to a red-hot blast of heat, and chuck in another shovel of

coal. If he ran low on water, he'd blow the steam whistle for the water monkey to fill the Reeves' side-mounted tanks. The whistle blasts were a kind of Morse code for communicating with the far-flung crew, so many toots for more coal and so many for more grain sacks. Neighbors who knew the code could tell what a crew was running short of just by listening for the whistle.

John stood atop the separator in a swirling cloud of chaff to supervise the unloading of bundles. It was the most important job, and also the dirtiest. A conveyor belt fed the bundles into a revolving cylinder with sawteeth that beat the kernels of grain out of the stalks. Inside the machine, separating tables winnowed grain from chaff while a fan blew the dust and straw out the wind stacker in a great rooster tail. A bundle tossed sideways or butt first onto the feeder would plug the cylinder and slow the belt until Berne gunned the throttle, the engine belching black smoke, but the grain would already be lost up the blower. When he wasn't astride the separator, John prowled around it, oiling the boxings and filling the grease cups, adjusting chains and pulleys, listening for trouble and trying to head it off. He checked the grain spout, where threshed oats poured into heavy linen sacks like a shower of gold. Three bushels to a sack. Before a sack was stitched and loaded onto a wagon to be driven to the granary, he dipped his hand inside, put a few kernels into his mouth, and chewed them to test their moisture before spitting them out.

Morning dragged on. The straw stack grew higher and higher, but the bundle wagons never stopped

Threshing day, then . . .

FACING PAGE, TOP: *A threshing crew and their Minneapolis Steel Machinery Company Twin City 12/20 tractor pause during threshing in the 1910s. MS&M also built its Twin City Twentieth Century tractor model specifically for the Grain Growers Co-op in Canada. (Minnesota Historical Society collection)*

. . . Threshing day, now

FACING PAGE, BOTTOM: *The belt is running during threshing day on an Old Order Amish farm in Lancaster County, Pennsylvania, in the 1990s. (Photograph by Keith Baum)*

Threshing outfit

OVERLEAF: *Threshing day of a bygone era: A threshing crew poses next to its steam traction engine in Stillwater, Minnesota, in 1922. (Photograph by John Runk/Minnesota Historical Society collection)*

Steam power

A restored 1926 steamer from the Keck, Gonnerman Company of Mt. Vernon, Indiana, on parade during the Rough and Tumble Threshermen's Reunion in Lancaster County, Pennsylvania. (Photograph by Keith Baum)

RAMBLINGS AT THE THRESHERMEN'S REUNION
By Ed Klimuska of Lancaster County, Pennsylvania

Instead of buying a vintage tractor, Roy Herr built one. "I just decided to marry the stuff and come up with a fun piece," Herr says.

Herr lives in East Petersburg, Pennsylvania, where he's been involved with farming, selling farm products like seeds and sheet metal fabrication all his life.

Herr built a steam tractor, which has an engine from this place, a chassis from that place, and a frame from another place. "I retired in 1987," he says. "By 1991, I had it to the point I could fire it and operate it."

He has a new tractor built from old parts. And, he takes his pride and joy to tractor shows in Pennsylvania.

"When I was a boy, I got hooked on steam," Herr says. "Three times steam was used on a farm. In the spring, it was used to sterilize tobacco beds. In the summer, it was used for threshing and bailing. That was a big event. In the late fall, it was used to shred corn into fodder. When the steam engine came, that was an event for us."

Herr bought his first tractor in 1947. It was made by Oliver. "It saved me work," he says. "It was a smooth-running machine. It was a six-cylinder, rather than a four-cylinder, engine."

coming. When they stopped bringing oats, they went on to barley, wheat, rye, and flax. Oats were the easiest to thresh, flax the hardest, especially if there was any moisture. Chaff from the blower dusted the spike pitchers with minstrel faces that cracked when they smiled. The sun beat down with no shade but the tatters of coal smoke drifting overhead. Some of the threshers munched green apples filched from the orchard and washed the sour taste down with cool water from a crock wrapped in burlap. John pulled his Elgin out of his pocket with increasing frequency. When it read 11:30, he gave the signal to shut down. Berne blew the whistle, then eased back on the throttle so the belt sagged to stop without slipping off the flywheel. The spike pitchers stabbed their pitchforks into the remaining bundles and headed across the field for the farmhouse in a long, ragged line.

Hearing the long whistle blast, Mame told the neighbor girl to hurry and finish setting the dining-room table. With four leaves added to accommodate the threshers, the table stretched from one wall to the next. Both women's faces were flushed, their hair hanging in damp ringlets, as they pulled crockery from the warming oven above the Jewel cookstove.

They could hear the men washing outside from a pail of water set out on the lawn. Now the crew stepped heavily onto the porch, the screen door slamming as they filed into the dining room and sat shoulder to shoulder, men and boys in sweat-stained overalls, sunburned except for blanched foreheads, their faces wet and shining with anticipation. Back and forth the women rushed from the kitchen, setting down platters of fried chicken or roast beef with gravy, bowls of mashed potatoes and rutabagas, fresh green beans, thick slices of bread with sweet butter, and gallons of hot coffee. A thresherman's wife was judged by the table she set, because the men she fed were not just hired hands but friends and neighbors. Mame would never think of serving mutton, as some wives did, and on Fridays she bought tins of salmon, which even the Protestants liked. The men barely spoke at first, so busy were they shoveling food into their mouths. They emptied their plates, refilled them, emptied them again. They ate in shifts, and as soon as one man left another took his place. Mame set down a half-dozen apple pies with golden, fluted crusts and slices of Cheddar cheese. Within minutes the pies vanished. Slowly, the last men stood up, nod-

ded to Mame, and staggered from the dining room to find some shade in the yard, leaving behind them the vast shambles of dinner.

Threshing continued into the evening until the last sack was filled or a heavy dew fell. Then the separator was hitched to the back of the tractor and hauled over the stubble fields and across the road to Sheehan's place. Some farmers wanted the straw piled in a field or blown into the barn, so the separator had to be placed accordingly and leveled. Berne would wheel the tractor around to face the separator, eyeballing it until flywheel and drivewheel were aligned to receive the belt. The last thing he did was bank the fire in the boiler so he could get up a head of steam the next morning. After Sheehan's farm, the crew moved down the road to Wileman's, Engles', McCoy's, St. George's, Portier's, Boardman's, Allen's, and Ryan's. For three months, the men spent their days at other farms and rode home each night to sleep in their own beds, so the threshing run itself resembled a long journey of stops and starts. By November the crew had traveled widely across most of two townships.

Every summer during threshing a caravan of Gypsies camped on the school grounds north of the farm. They arrived in canvas-covered wagons and stayed until the urge to move again struck or the law ran them off. Sometimes the men would drift into the grain fields to trade horses or borrow a tool. They were swarthy men, very serious, and their horses were always very fine. The women came later. Wearing layers of brightly colored rags, they cordoned themselves behind a ring of snot-nosed children and begged unabashedly. Usually they begged grain for their horses and went away if they got it. Once a thresher refused and a short time later noticed a very fat Gypsy woman loping oddly from his grain wagon. He sent some boys running after her. As they chased her across the field, something the size of a small child dropped from beneath her skirts: a full sack of oats. The woman kept running.

The next morning the school yard was empty; the Gypsy caravan had struck camp, and, in a little while, so did the threshers. What would it be like, a thresher might ask himself as he rattled down the road to the next farm, to live that way, like a Gypsy, traveling all the time with no place to call home but the stars overhead and the great, wide world beneath your feet?

SAWYER MASSEY

HAMILTON CANADA

PATENTED
FEB 12 1892
JULY 11 1895
L666

JUDSON
GOVERNOR
CO
ROCHESTER N.Y.

Threshing

By Ed Klimuska

Ed Klimuska has Pennsylvania bred in his bones. Born in Wilkes-Barre, he has lived in Lancaster County for some twenty-five years now, writing for the Lancaster *New Era* newspaper on farming, rural life, and, especially, on the Amish, for which he was honored by the Anabaptist Center of Elizabethtown College.

In this essay, he writes about several Old Order Amish farmers who are drawn to preserve the steam tractors and threshing machines of their youth.

Eli Smucker stood on the back end of a big, old steam engine shoveling coal into a firebox to power a threshing rig.

Smucker lives in Lancaster County, Pennsylvania, a progressive farming community with 4,500 family-owned farms. One of the top producing farm counties in the United States, Lancaster County has a rich agricultural heritage that stretches back nearly three hundred years.

With his yesteryear machinery and equipment, Smucker has brought back a piece of that heritage rarely seen in the fast-paced world of agriculture where farmers grasp technological advances to stay ahead. Helped by family and friends, he harvested wheat like it was done in the late 1800s and early 1900s.

"This just brings back old-day memories," Smucker says.

Once farmers used threshing machines to thresh or separate kernels of grain from stalks. Before threshers came on the scene, farmers threshed and winnowed by hand—a hard and slow task. Threshers increased efficiency. The earliest threshers were powered by horses walking a treadmill. Then, steam engines replaced the horses. Since the 1930s, combines have done the work.

Smucker belongs to the Old Order Amish Church whose farmers do field work with horse-drawn equipment. But even Amish farmers don't use steam-powered threshing machines as a regular part of their agricultural practices. When they take to their fields with steam-driven threshers, they're reaching into an agricultural past mostly for fun or what Smucker calls "memories."

In a week's time, Smucker and his crew of eight men and boys harvested eighteen acres of wheat, or 1,400 bushels, from four nearby farms. Threshing is a social experience among the Amish, neighbors helping neighbors with chores.

Smucker's steam-engine was built in 1922 by a Pennsylvania company. Now retired from farming, Smucker keeps busy by restoring steam engines, going to threshermen's reunions, and using his steam engine once a year to harvest wheat. "I do the threshing, and I'm the fireman," he says.

Threshing wheat with a steam-powered engine is a rare sight these days. As the crew did its job along a rural road in the hot July sun, scores of people stopped their cars, got out, did a double take, and wondered

Steamer details

Details from an 1890s Sawyer-Massey steam traction engine from the Sawyer-Massey Company of Hamilton, Ontario. Sawyer-Massey was one of the main Canadian steam and gasoline tractor builders from the 1860s through the 1920s, competing with the other major pioneering Canadian manufacturer, Goold, Shapley & Muir Company of Brantford, Ontario. Although Sawyer-Massey shared distribution with Massey-Harris, the two firms were not related. (Photograph by Jerry Irwin)

what was going on. Many took pictures. "They've never seen anything like this," Smucker says. "If I advertised this, the crowd would be so big it wouldn't be fit to walk around."

Smucker remembers when his father used steam-driven threshers. "Years ago, every farmer had wheat," he says. Today, field corn, which is fed to farm animals, and hay make up the bulk of acres on Lancaster County farms.

Threshing is hard and dirty work. But the hardest part might be keeping the parts functioning in the old rigs and engines. Smucker puts it this way: "It is something to keep all those belts, to take care of them, and to see the thing keeps running. We need belt power. The steam engine drives the belt, which runs the machine. The wheat goes right through the machine. We call it a separator. It shakes the wheat right out. This brings back great memories—but it's hard work."

Horses hitched to wagons bring the wheat from the fields to the barn area where the threshing is done. The steam-engine is a big machine that huffs and puffs. When it builds up too much pressure, the engine's pop-off valve blows. Neither the steam nor the noise scares the horses whose presence enhances the yesteryear appeal of the threshing experience.

Lancaster County farmers have strong and happy memories of the old days when threshing crews were common neighborhood groups. David Fisher is one of them. "It was hard but we always had a ball," he says. "A rig did six farms. We helped each other. We always had a good time."

What Fisher recalls the best is when the wheat harvest was over near the end of July. The farmers had a settling party. They met on a farm, breathed a sigh of relief, and relaxed. They ate hot dogs, watermelons, and ice cream. They had cold drinks. They pitched horseshoes. And, they settled their financial accounts by paying the owner of the rig. Fisher says the settling party was usually on the property of the farmer who got the most bushels per acre.

Farmer Samuel Stoltzfus also has vivid memories of threshing. "When I was a little chap, we used to thresh with steam engines," Stoltzfus says. "Joe King was the engineer. He'd crawl up in his steam engine, fill his mouth with chew tobacco, fill up the firebox and say, "Fingers out." Then, he would blow the whistle—*toot, toot*. Then, he'd open the throttle. It would go chug, and the belt would flap."

Stoltzfus worked at steam-powered threshing until fifteen years ago. Now, it's a dying trade practiced by only a handful of Old Order Amish or Old Order Mennonite families. They sow the wheat in the fall, and it's ready for harvest after the Fourth of July.

"It's hard work and there's no money in it," Stoltzfus says. "Wheat prices are about a dollar less than the 1950s. With the prices we get for alfalfa and corn, it doesn't pay to raise wheat. Wheat was a cash crop. Some farmers kept a ton or two. Usually, it was all sold to mills. A lot was shipped outside of Lancaster County. Handling all those wheat bags was sort of gut work. We handled one-hundred-pound wheat bags. The guys got so tired they didn't care. Now, they blow it in a truck."

Stoltzfus says wheat was a great cash crop. With the wheat check, farmers paid fertilizer bills and rent. "Wheat could almost be a sure crop, dry weather or not," Stoltzfus adds.

Because threshing wheat was hard work in hot, often humid, weather, the farmers worked up hearty appetites. "It took three ladies to cook," Stoltzfus says. "The most important ingredient of all was dinner, supper, and the evening snack. We always tried to work a little fast so we could catch up and have a little rest."

The wheat harvest was the high mark of summer. In Stoltzfus's words: "I loved it. It was like the Taj Mahal of farm work. It lasted long enough. It just lasted the right amount of time that you all had a lot of fun. It wasn't harder than any other kind of farm work. It was hot, sweaty, and dirty. It took a lot of chewing tobacco. I miss it."

Kerosene power

ABOVE: *The Advance-Rumely Thresher Company of LaPorte, Indiana, debuted its famous Rumely OilPull in 1910, as a lightweight, kerosene-powered alternative to the monstrous steam traction engines that were the state of the art at the time. In its various horsepower ratings, the OilPull was a popular tractor in the United States and, especially, Canada. But a Canadian crop failure in 1914 left the company over-leveraged on new tractor sales, and the grand old firm went into receivership—only to be reborn, this time without the Rumely family. This 1923 OilPull Model G is owned by Scott Thompson of Tremont, Illinois. (Photograph by Ralph W. Sanders)*

Threshing Wheat

OVERLEAF: *American artist Thomas Hart Benton painted this evocative image of a threshing day in 1938–1939, using oil and tempura on canvas. Benton was a native of Kansas, and many of his impressionistic paintings, with their swirling imagery and curvaceous lines, depict the American heartland. (© T. H. Benton and R. P. Benton Testamentary Trusts/Licensed by VAGA, New York, NY; The Sheldon Swope Art Gallery, Terre Haute, Indiana)*

THRESHING MEAL MENU
By Edna Lester of Hamilton, Ohio

My mother was one of those who prided herself on the culinary arts. The main course of meat usually consisted of roast capon, baked ham, roast beef, to which would be added mounds of mashed potatoes, potato salad, sugared sweet potatoes, fresh peas, right from the family garden. To this would be added applesauce, strawberry preserves, currant and grape jellies, that had been so carefully prepared months before for just such an occasion. All these good things would be topped off with pies galore: apple, peach, berry, gooseberry, and a half-dozen kinds of cake.

The Last Threshing

By Sara De Luca

Dancing the Cows Home: A Wisconsin Girlhood is Sara De Luca's memoir of growing up on her family's farm near Milltown, Wisconsin, from her birth in 1943 through her adolescence in the 1950s. Sara tells of her hard-working, stout-hearted Norwegian-American mother and her Danish-American father, who felt enslaved by the land and cattle; she writes of the hardships of farming as well as the joys, of the struggles as well as the triumphs. In sum, however, her story is one of memories as rich as the fertile land. She explains in the book that she wrote her memoir because she was seeking "to climb back inside those fences to a time and place that felt like home."

This excerpt tells of all the activities of threshing day—and to the final days of a way of life.

A sharply focused, black-and-white snapshot captures Teddy and me playing near the weathered granary. I know the bull-thistles, the tall quack, the curving tines of a hayrake parked in the left corner. I know the hulking metal monster that stands in the background. This is the threshing machine—a Nichols and Shepard Red River Special. It stands fifteen feet tall and measures forty-five feet head to tail, from the front-end feeder housing to the bonnet on the blower pipe. Its spike-toothed cylinders can digest a field of oats in one voracious afternoon. This is a dinosaur on the eve of its extinction. The photograph is dated on the back—August 1955—the season of our last threshing.

This threshing beast knew many fields and many masters. It was too costly and cumbersome for one farmer to own and operate. Neighbors pooled their labor and resources, buying one machine to serve eight or ten farms. As summer waned, they gathered around someone's kitchen table and drew up a schedule as fairly and sensibly as possible.

"Let's see, Ed, you were first last year so we'll have to put you farther down the line."

"Lyle's oats are nearly ripe, and his shocks stood through three hard rains last year—we ought to start with him."

Each prayed for fine weather when the creature came lumbering onto his land. The cutting, binding, and shocking had been done in advance; golden tepees of oats stood pitched in the field, dry and ripe and ready for the final phase of harvest.

Now, from sunup to sundown the bundles were hauled in and fed to the ravenous machine, which rumbled and groaned as it separated the precious kernels from their dry, dusty stems. Chaff and straw were spit high into the air, raining down all day to form a shiny golden stack. The precious straw would serve as bedding for the cattle throughout their long winter confinement in the barn.

We girls were not allowed to hang around the noisy, dangerous equipment. Little Priscilla, only five, was not allowed outdoors at all. Yet our brother at the age of nine ran freely behind the wagons and perched on the fender of the laboring John Deere tractor that powered the giant machine. We girls kept busy in the kitchen all morning, peeling tubs of potatoes and carrots, snapping beans, stirring jugs of Kool-Aid, setting the table for ten hungry men who would appear promptly when the noon whistle blew in town.

Ghost

The ghost of a McCormick-Deering tractor haunts a farm meadow. (Photograph by Andy Kraushaar)

It was a hearty, hasty feast, not long on conversation. When the crew had emptied their plates and pushed their chairs back from the table, there were piles of dirty dishes, pots, and pans to wash and dry. No time for lunch or recess. We nibbled on the leavings as we cleaned up the mess. Mama warned us to be quick—it was nearly time to prepare afternoon lunches. Sandwiches and fresh fruits and cake and hand-squeezed lemonade must be boxed and bagged and toted to the fields by three o'clock.

This picnic was our favorite part of threshing day. The men relaxed under a shade tree and shared a round of ethnic jokes—in which the Norwegians generally got the best of the poor dumb Swedes—and some good-natured teasing and horseplay. Peggy, Susie, and I were noticed for the first time all day. ("How tall and pretty those girls are getting to be! And such a good help in the kitchen. They'll make fine farm wives some day, no doubt about that!")

With luck and fair weather, the oats were stored safely in the bins by twilight, and the sweaty crew was gone, tending to their own pressing chores at home. The threshing rig was hauled off down the road and readied for its next assignment.

When it was all over Daddy sank into his favorite chair without bothering to empty the cuffs of his overalls or brush away the chaff that had settled on his bushy brows.

"It was a bumper crop, a good ninety bushels to the acre," he reported on threshing night, 1955, "and it went like clockwork. Will you look at that strawstack! That's got to be the highest stack of good clean straw this farm has ever seen!"

It seemed to me he said that every year. Daddy always took great satisfaction in bringing in a healthy crop of oats. The strawstack stood like a gigantic monument to his achievement. Two years before—in 1953, when I was ten and Teddy seven—we celebrated by climbing to the top of the slippery mountain and flinging ourselves down, over and over again, until the stack was pocked with craters.

Daddy had been furious. "Damn it to hell!" he had exploded. "That strawstack wasn't settled! You kids have torn it up so bad—the rain will run straight through and *rot the whole damn stack!*"

He hadn't spanked us, although we certainly deserved it. The look on his face served as my punishment. I would never make that kind of mischief again,

and I would see that Teddy didn't, either.

Daddy was gone right after milking to join the crew at Vollrath's farm a half mile down the road.

My sisters and I were ready for a quiet day, but our little brother—not quite old enough to join the men—was bored and restless. The sudden stillness was more than he could bear. At midday Mama sent me to investigate what Teddy was up to. I discovered him huddled over a pile of kindling, a sack of marshmallows in one hand and a fistful of kitchen matches in the other. He was obviously preparing for a roast.

"Mama and Daddy have told you a million times not to play with fire!" I screamed.

"It's okay, Sara," he assured me. "I'm making my fire on this sandy spot right under the gas barrels."

I snatched the matches from his hand and marched him to the house where Mama delivered a fierce lecture and a swat across the butt.

It was not enough. A couple of hours later, I found Teddy playing quietly near the strawstack. Using a clipper clothespin, he had invented a device that would strike a match and shoot it high into the air in one swift operation. I was seconds too late. Teddy's latest aim had gone awry, shooting his match into the mantle of straw surrounding the stack. The light flared and raced like a tiny river, winding, licking over the ground. He tried to stamp it out, but the lapping stream was becoming a swift current, tunneling through open channels toward the hot, thirsty center of the stack.

Teddy grabbed a stick and whacked the flames. A plume of dark smoke spiraled upward, warning us that no amount of stamping or pounding would suffice.

I ran for the telephone and rang Central—one short, desperate turn of the crank—yelling "*Fire! Fire at the Hellerud farm!*"

The town siren wailed almost instantly. Soon two red fire engines clanged up the drive, followed by a growling yellow water tanker. Men leaped from the trucks, rolled out their hoses, and aimed them into the inferno. The wind was rising; torrents of water had almost no effect upon the towering flames. The weather vane mounted on the barn roof swirled wildly as the wind shifted to the southwest, gained force and speed, then shifted due south, blowing the burning straw straight toward the barn.

THRESHING MEAL ADVICE
From the *Farmer's Guide*, 1916

The threshing meal is said an old-time custom, and custom is a hard task master. While most women see that it is a foolish practice they fear being thought lazy or lacking in means if they don't come up to their neighbor in setting a groaning table. Now we all know that a lazy woman in the country is as scarce as the proverbial needle in the hay stack and everybody in the country has an abundance to eat, but time and bodily strength to do what is required of them are what they lack. . . . When the men form their threshing rings, let the women also form a ring to consider the threshing dinner. Cold lunches have been tried but no one relishes a cold lunch. A simple, wholesome meal would be appreciated by the workers in the field. Let some more leisurely time be the occasion for the elaborate and intricate menus.

Harvest lunch

The John A. Johnson family rests for lunch in the shade of a haystack during the harvest in Nicollet County, Minnesota, in 1907. (Minnesota Historical Society collection)

Threshing time, then . . .
ABOVE: *Threshing on the Northcote, Minnesota, farm of James J. Hill, circa 1900. Hill was the railroad tycoon of Great Northern fame. (Minnesota Historical Society collection)*

. . . Ghosts of threshing days past
RIGHT: *The rusted remains of past threshing days rest in peace. (Photograph by Jerry Irwin)*

A Bad Name for Threshing Meals
By Edna Lester of Hamilton, Ohio

Sometimes a stingy housewife would skimp on the beef or pork and slip in some wieners, which we held in low repute. She got a bad name if she tried it too often.

THRESHING DAY
By Sara De Luca of Amery, Wisconsin

Early each autumn a gigantic monster named
  McCormick-Deering
crawled up our driveway, pulled by a growling green John
  Deere.
Grain spout, straw blower pipe, feed apron had been
  folded for the ride,
belts rolled and stored inside its empty belly. Even in
  sleep,
it crushed small stones beneath its iron feet.

Unfolding and awakening with furious appetite,
the dinosaur brought chomping, wheezing, banging
  climax
to a season of relentless work and worry. A crew of seven
  sweaty men
dismantled golden shocks, hauled bundles from the
  sun-baked field,
and pitched them toward the gaping maw.
The creature spit back polished oats; its bowels
  thundered
as they blew out sweet clean straw.

September 1953, my brother Teddy—eight years old—
  climbed topside,
rode there like a king trembling with power. He reigned
for minutes only,
soon dethroned by angry shouts and shaking fists.
Daddy and his neighbor held a spongy stance atop the
  bundle wagon,
one misstep from frightful jaws and hacking teeth.
They laughed and yelled above the din, not caring
that they perched so near the end of life.
Daddy jumped down, hauled himself beneath the drive belt
for a quick inspection as it squealed and whined, a deadly
  bandsaw,
inches from his head. "Belt started slipping! Shut 'er down
  for now—
It's time to eat!"

They gathered in, mopping red necks and brows with their
  bandannas,
spilling chaff from cuffs and pockets.
"Now that's a damned fine crop, wouldn't you say?"
"You betcha! Nearly ninety bushels to the acre!"
Mama hurried from the stove with mashed potatoes,
  steaming stew.
I followed after with the rhubarb pie and ice cream, strangely
  shy,
silenced this day by scenes of glory and disaster.

Two firemen tugged on the ropes that hoisted the haymow door, hoping to shield the mow full of dry hay from fiery arrows of straw that sailed on the wind. The men hosed down the barn with great geysers pumped from the tanker, soaking the wooden shingles. Somehow they would have to hold the firebomb below its flash point.

By now Daddy and some members of the threshing crew had joined the firemen. "I don't know if we can get ahead of it with the tankers, Harvey," a fireman said, shaking his helmeted head. "Okay if we start pumping water from your well?"

"Do what you have to," Daddy answered in a shaky voice.

The battle raged all afternoon and into the evening. Mama and Peggy milked the cows inside the threatened barn while Susie and I ran back and forth with sandwiches and Thermoses of coffee for the hungry men, who swallowed them down without even wiping the soot from their hands and faces.

At dusk I noticed a string of cars and pickups lining the gravel road that ran past the farm. A couple of vehicles had even driven into the yard. Their occupants wandered into the denuded oat field; some were milling curiously around the buildings, staring at the strawstack, shielding their eyes against the searing blaze. It was a shocking invasion, more startling than the fire. I saw the fury in Mama's eyes. "Some folks don't have enough to do," is all she said. We were too busy to bother with idle spectators. Gradually they meandered away.

Night fell and still the flames smoldered and flickered back to life. The strawstack shed water like an umbrella, and no amount of dousing could penetrate its burning core. The firemen claimed they had pumped fifteen thousand gallons of water on the stack, and still it burned like a bog of peat. Around midnight a great swiveling crane equipped with a toothed bucket gulped the straw and spewed it out in all directions. A bulldozer finished the job, scattering the soggy remains of Daddy's strawstack far and wide across the scarred pasture.

Teddy watched from an upstairs window, his sisters' arms around him. There was no need to hide—some crimes are too enormous to be punished.

Next morning the cattle surveyed the blackened area in confusion. Hot spots still smoked and flared.

"What will the cows do for bedding when winter comes?" Teddy asked in a small, trembling voice.

"I don't know, Teddy. I just don't know," I answered.

I didn't know, either, that this mountain of amber stems that stood so briefly in the August sunlight would be the last.

It was our final threshing. The next year a modern combine harvested Daddy's crop directly in the field, cutting and threshing the oats all in one efficient operation. A baler came behind to pack and bind the straw for storage under cover in the mow. The crews were disbanded; it was every man for himself. There were no more buckets of potatoes to be peeled, no more lemonade to tote on threshing day. And in a small yet telling way, our world was changed forever.

Chapter 4

Homage to the Mechanical Mule

"I have not heard many farmers rhapsodize about machines, except perhaps for ones they used during childhood—two-cylinder Deere tractors or one of the early Farmalls."
—Verlyn Klinkenborg, Making Hay

Rhapsodizing about machines may not be in a farmer's nature, but when the conversation turns to old tractors that have stood the test of time on a farm, sit back and get ready for a long story. Tales told of good tractors—like stories of faithful horses or good crop yields—take on the character of an homage.

The reminiscences here are all devoted to specific makes of tractor that have somehow, for some reason, made one farmer a true believer.

Mechanical mule, then . . .
LARGE PHOTO: *An International Harvester Farmall F-20 pulls a McCormick-Deering harvester. (Photograph by J. C. Allen and Son)*

. . . Mechanical mule, now
INSET: *A restored International Harvester Cub from the Antique Gas & Steam Engine Museum in Vista, California. (Photograph by Vincent Manocchi)*

One Author's Beginnings

By Don Macmillan

Englishman Don Macmillan is the dean of John Deere historians. Don has been involved in all aspects of vintage and new farm tractors: He started as a farmer before becoming a Deere dealer, and has since become a well-known collector of vintage tractors, an active member of the English branch of the Two-Cylinder Club, and the foremost chronicler of John Deere. His books include the landmark *John Deere Tractors and Equipment* volumes one and two, *John Deere Albums* volumes one and two, and *John Deere Tractors Worldwide*.

In this reminiscence, Don salutes the tractors that have influenced his life.

In the late 1930s, I was working on a 640-acre Cotswold sheep farm, ten miles (16 km) from Gloucester, where we had one Allis-Chalmers B tractor. All of the rest of the work was done with horses, as well as the annual visit of the steam threshing outfit.

I learned to plow with three horses and a two-furrow walking plow (no sulky plows in the United Kingdom in those days!), milk cows by hand as we had two herds (one a pedigree Friesian [Holstein]), make ricks of sheaves and thatch them against our wet weather, build stone walls, and shear sheep. It was bad luck on the sheep.

When World War II began, the government required us to plow up more land, so we ordered a new Allis-Chalmers WF, similar to one we borrowed occasionally from a brother-in-law. The Cotswold farmer's brother had a son who knew his tractors; he had ordered a John Deere AR.

Both tractors were a long time coming, and, in the end, the brother was offered a Minneapolis-Moline U, which he accepted. Almost at once, the AR turned up in Gloucester, so he phoned us to see if we would like it. My boss agreed that if it would pull a three-furrow up a steep bank we were about to reclaim, we would have it.

When the dealer brought it out to our farm, I was delegated to do the demonstration, a task it performed easily. Not only did it pull the three-furrow Cockshutt plow with ease, I even persuaded the farmer subsequently to buy a four-furrow. Everyone was amazed at the pulling power of this relatively small tractor when compared with the local 15-30 and W-30 International models popular locally. So instead of a commitment to the orange, I became an enthusiast for the green and yellow.

Despite this change of allegiance, there was another pull toward the orange, one that started my second chief interest in my farming life. We were one of the first farms to have a combine harvester, a 5-foot-cut (150-cm) Allis-Chalmers 60 PTO-driven bagger

"Aces All"

This 1924 Deere calendar image showed a youngster driving his Deere Model D with a No. 5 plow and waving to an airplane and its pilot. The title of the image, "Aces All," tied together farmers with the heroic aviators of the 1920s. (Deere & Company archives)

of the early type, with the round-top to the straw-walker hood. Again, the AR proved as good on the PTO as the drawbar.

On the gas tank of the new tractor it said John Deere, Moline, Illinois. So I wrote to John Deere, Moline, Illinois, and said what a fabulous tractor we had with the AR. They wrote back and said when the war was over I must come and visit.

In the fall of 1947, I made the first of some twenty-three trips so far to the United States, visiting all the major tractor makers, in addition to my visit to Moline, Waterloo, and Dubuque. I visited Allis-Chalmers, Caterpillar, International, and M-M; of the major manufacturers, I missed out only on Oliver.

Prior to this, in August 1942, I had started contract plowing on my own account through the British War Agricultural Committees. It proved impossible to find a secondhand John Deere, so I bought an Oliver 90 on rubbers, a Ransomes four-furrow plow, and a fuel tender with a rear platform for my motorcycle.

I was sent initially to Chipping Camden in Gloucestershire, but the heavy clay ground proved impossible to plow with the War Ag's crawlers or even with the steel-wheeled Oliver, so after a trip to Dorset where the ground was the same, I ended up in Wiltshire where I have been ever since. I had so much work for my outfit, machinery being scarce, that I ordered a new John Deere D, and on February 8, 1943, I became the proud owner of serial number 154757, my first John Deere, for £415 on steels, about $1,660. With another driver, we were inundated with work, and farmers asked me, as a contractor journeying about, to find them different machines.

In 1944, I bought my first combine, my second love after John Deere tractors, a Case QRS 12-foot (360-cm) bagger with the C engine. Again, so much combining was booked that I had to buy a second, an M-M JR 6-foot (180-cm) PTO machine that we pulled with the D. By then, I had four John Deere tractors: another used unstyled D, a used unstyled BW, and a new A that was delivered just before harvest on steels, which we used to pull the Case.

After harvest, I decided I could not afford to keep two combines and advertised the M-M for sale. As soon as it was sold, for £10 more than it had cost, I was inundated with requests for combines. I even sold the Case as well, having discovered that I could purchase machines just before using them and sell them afterwards for a profit. And so started my career as a dealer.

Early in 1947, before my trip to the United States, I purchased a 220-acre arable farm to occupy the contracting staff when they were not busy. Two years later, a grass drier (dehydrator) was installed in the barn, which made farming more interesting in the summertime. We harvested special grasses and alfalfa from May to late fall.

During the 1947 American trip, the directors of the Jack Olding and Frank Standen companies, importers of John Deere machines for the south and east of England, respectively, both purchased a new 55 12-foot (360-cm) combine with sacker attachment. When these both became secondhand in 1953, I purchased them, converting one to a tanker for use on my farm. I still own both; they are with a friend who hopes to restore one of the two.

Olding's directors accompanied me on the way over to the United States for my first visit. We flew in an American Airlines Super Constellation, a four-engined plane with triple tailfin, calling at Shannon in Ireland for dinner, and at Gander, Newfoundland, for refueling. Leaving London at 3:30 P.M., we arrived next morning in New York about 8:00.

In order to see one of the new 55 self-propelled combines at work, I had to travel from Moline to Champaign, Illinois, and spend the day with the local Deere dealer and two brothers who owned the machine.

In the evening, waiting at the station for a bus to Peoria, I got into a conversation with a guy who had married an English girl from Charlton, near Kingsbridge in Devon. She was the daughter of a pub owner there, a hostelry I knew!

He insisted that I come home with him to meet his wife. In the end, I stayed the night, and the couple and two of their friends took me to Peoria the next day in their Packard. Further, the next weekend was the big football game between Illinois and Minnesota, and so I *had to* come down again from Chicago for the weekend. It was all an enjoyable interlude in my six-week tour.

Instead of returning home on the Queen Elizabeth, and due entirely to the great hospitality of all I met, I delayed a week and joined the Queen Mary. This, too, was fortunate, as Frank Standen and his son, Peter, were on the same ship, and it was then I

Minnie Moline
With "Best wishes for a prosperous 1939," Minnie Moline signed promotional pinup photographs of herself sitting astride the latest offering from Minne-Mo. This Minneapolis-Moline archival picture notes that the tractor here is a UDLX, although without its famous enclosed cab. (Minnesota Historical Society collection)

learned they had arranged to import the second 55 for a farmer in Huntingdonshire.

By 1948, I was operating eight combines and three pickup balers on custom work, in addition to my own harvest. After the pound sterling was devalued against the dollar in 1950 from $4 to the pound to $2.80, all Deere machines became too expensive to import. One result of this was that we never had the Numbered Series of two-cylinder tractors in the United Kingdom.

In 1958, I sold 112 combines, mostly used, possibly a record for one person. And for several years, I passed the eighty mark. In the same year I was appointed the first John Deere dealer in the United Kingdom.

In the context of combines, during my second visit to the United States in 1959, I was able to purchase one of the new 95 Hi-Lo tanker combines. I wanted one with a 12-foot (360-cm) cut, but was told the smallest available was 14-foot (420-cm). By searching various books, I was able to point out that, by ordering a

combine with draper header less the pickup unit, and adding a 55 12-foot cutting mechanism, the problem was solved.

The reason for my visit in 1959 was the last great show of two-cylinder 30 Series tractors and machinery put on by Deere at Marshalltown, Iowa. I was able to drive an 830 with six-furrow drawn plow with hydraulic lift, and appreciated the potential of this largest and last of the two-cylinder line.

It was here that Deere introduced the 8010 and its eight-furrow integral plow to the amazement (and confusion?) of the farmers present. With its wide sweep when the plow was raised, stewards were necessary at each end of the field to protect the crowd. Finally, everyone wondered what this strange new model-numbering system—eight zero one zero—meant?

In addition to the tractors, the new Hi-Lo combines were shown for the first time, plus a new, small, self-propelled Model 40 with either an 8- or 10-foot

(240- or 300-cm) grain head, or a two-row corn head.

At home in January 1959, I had bought two tractors that were to become the nucleus of my collection of vintage John Deeres, using them for many years on my farm. The only Model R imported to the British Isles, serial number 4661, was delivered by the importers to a contractor in Dublin, and I managed to purchase it as its second owner. While in Ireland, I also bought a Model M, serial number 14021, several of which were delivered over there, though none came to the United Kingdom.

Three other tractors that I purchased in 1962 in Ireland, two of them new, that were not originally imported to the United Kingdom, but were sent to the Emerald Isle, were John Deere-Lanz 500s, the first John Deere New Generation model produced in Mannheim, Germany, from January 1960, eight months before the Dallas, Texas, announcement of the new models.

It was also in 1962 that the 4010 and 5010 tractors were announced at the December Smithfield Show in London, giving us new John Deere tractors to sell for the first time since 1950.

Over the years, I was able to build up my collection to more than thirty tractors, including a Waterloo Boy N and a spoke D, both purchased in Canada. Other nice tractors I found for my collection were an unstyled L, serial number 621777, from Michigan, and the only BNH I have on my JD register.

After twenty-two years as a Deere dealer, and with a depression signaled, I decided to retire in 1980, and sold my two dealerships to my neighboring Deere dealer. In order to sell all the two-cylinder parts — which I had acquired when Standen gave up John Deere due to lack of supply of new machines — and also the transport vehicles that the new owner did not want, I called a sale, with the vintage collection as the draw.

In England, one can put a reserve price on any machine in a sale in case it doesn't make the required price. I had intended to sell a few of the tractors and keep most of the others, but the sale was so good that I only ended up with ten left, plus four others still in North America awaiting shipment.

English Fordson

Henry Ford's Fordson was famous in the United States and Canada, as well as Great Britain and the rest of Europe. This 1937 Model N was built in Dagenham, Essex, Great Britain, during the production run from 1933 to 1946, and exported back to American and Canadian markets. Owner: Eric Coates of Southampton, Hampshire, Great Britain. (Photograph by Andrew Morland)

Allis-Chalmers tractors, then . . .

RIGHT: *Oat harvest: An Allis-Chalmers WC works a binder cutting oats on the Willard Capes farm near Kintland, Indiana, in 1935. (Photograph by J. C. Allen and Son)*

. . . Allis-Chalmers tractors, now

BELOW: *A beautifully restored 1938 Allis-Chalmers WC with a wide front end. Owner: Steve Rosenboom of Pomeroy, Iowa. (Photograph by Ralph W. Sanders)*

Workhorses

A weathered barn in Rothsville, Pennsylvania, houses a duo of well-used tractor workhorses and a New Holland implement. (Photograph by Keith Baum)

These fourteen provided the nucleus for a second collection that again mounted into the high twenties, most of which were loaned to our Science Museum, and kept at its storage place on a local, inactive aerodrome. Eventually, the museum lost its curator, and the director of transport, who replaced him, decided they had too many tractors of one make; so I sold all but four to other collectors, as I had nowhere to store them by then.

This brings me to my retirement and the 1980s. A friend who was familiar with a couple of albums on John Deere tractors for Allan Condie in the United Kingdom was asked by people at the American Society of Agricultural Engineers whether he knew anyone who would be interested in writing the history of

John Deere Tractors and Equipment. He kindly thought of me.

Another trip to the United States early in 1988, to the ASAE head office in Michigan and to Moline for a meeting with Deere vice-president Chet Lascelles, as well as Deere's marketing director, librarian, archivist, and ex-editor of *The Furrow*, resulted in the necessary approval to proceed.

When I asked why the largest farm machinery company in the world, and American to boot, was agreeing to an Englishman writing their history, Chet said simply, "Welcome aboard!" I had been aboard for the previous forty-eight years. And now as I write this, and am in the middle of my fourth book, this time for Voyageur Press, the score has risen to fifty-seven.

Oliver tractors, then . . .

ABOVE: *Lined up against a Farmall M, an Oliver 60 Row Crop prepares for a corn harvesting contest in the 1940s. (Photograph by J. C. Allen and Son)*

. . . Oliver tractors, now

LEFT: *An obviously well-used Oliver 77 Row Crop rests alongside a barn bearing an Oliver dealer sign. The Oliver Corporation of Chicago, Illinois, was a stalwart manufacturer of farm tractors from its formation in 1929 until it was acquired by the White Motor Corporation of Oak Brook, Illinois, in 1960. White also purchased Cockshutt of Canada in 1962, and added its tractors as a subsidiary of the Oliver line. (Photograph by Jerry Irwin)*

THE MOTOR CONTEST
By L. W. Ellis and Edward A. Rumely,
Power and the Plow, 1911

Clouds of smoke and hissing steam; a broad prairie stretching for miles without a break, save for the distant mirage; here and there a tiny prairie fire held in leash by bands of blackened earth; dust and heat; throngs of eager spectators; the song of vibrant steel and the cracking roots of age-old sod—imagine all this, add to it the sight of a score of monster engines pulling leviathan plows, and you have a faint picture of the Winnipeg plowing contest. Shining prows of steel, cleaving the waves of a sea of prairie grass; long furrows lost in a haze; lines of fluttering flags to guide the engineer on a straight course; huge twenty-ton engines mere dots on the landscape, and you have the impression of distance. Refreshment tents, excursion trains, busy autos running errands for the slow-moving tractors, or whisking the manufacturer's crew back and forth, and you feel the spirit of a modern festival. Then, in the twilight, mild-eyed cattle meandering slowly over the upturned field, wondering, Rip Van Winkle-like, at the transformation, and you sense a tragedy, for the pasture of the ox and buffalo from time immemorial is lost forever to advancing civilization. In the night, when the camps have vanished, one might even fancy Indian spirits floating miserably over the desolate waste of a one-time happy hunting ground.

What is this affair? It is an annual contest, a feature of the Winnipeg Industrial Exhibition, open to the world for either steam or internal-combustion tractors of any size or weight. The contest of 1908, first of its kind on the American continent, was received with skepticism, admixed with wonder, but the world-wide interest in the results proved the timeliness of such a demonstration of the utility of mechanical power on the farm. With succeeding competitions this interest has in nowise abated, and the present scene is the crowning event of them all.

Morning mist
Early morning fog dissipates in the warmth of the sun rising over Pennsylvania farmland. (Photograph by Jerry Irwin)

8N-Joyment

By Gerard W. Rinaldi

Gerard Rinaldi is the publisher of the *9N-2N-8N Newsletter* and a devoted Ford N Series tractor fan. His magazine is a stylish and informative club publication that keeps members up-to-date on all things relating to Ford tractors.

In this essay, Gerard describes how the restoration and use of his Ford 8N tractor taught him new things about himself.

What exactly are the pleasures of owning an old tractor, in keeping it running well and looking good? When I'm up in the operator's seat, letting my forty-six-year-old machine do what it does best, that's when I contemplate that question.

First of all, the seat of almost any tractor is a place unbelievably conducive to meditating, if you haven't yet realized it. Perhaps one day I'll offer a sequel to Robert Pirsig's popular novel. Will there be a call for *Zen and the Art of Tractor Maintenance?*

It takes some concentration to keep the old tractors running, but not too much. They seem to oblige with an unusual willingness to perform, and with a constitution not often found in many of our products today: They never featured planned obsolescence. It still pleasantly surprises me each time my old Ford 8N leaps to attention, like an old dog that is ready for a romp, despite any ills of age, even in the dead of winter.

In our ambiance of bubble-pack, squash-down, throwaway living, there is both a convenience and a bolstered economy in which we all benefit somehow. It is a curious game of paradox.

But there is another game I enjoy as well. To win, one must perform the trick of keeping the oldest things useful and working well as long as possible and by the most energy-efficient and cost-effective means possible. That's marathon talk. The real competition is with oneself, to get in shape, to maintain that tone, to plan ahead, to work carefully and efficiently, and to pace all efforts. With such an attitude, I restored a tractor and depend on its usefulness today.

These thoughts go back more than thirty years, when I began teaching art subjects in the public school of a community that was still quite rural. Although times would change, haying was common on several small farms nearby, supporting the many horse enthusiasts. One of my students, David, a high schooler unusually well informed about tractors, had an uncanny ability to name the make and model from great distances, when only a tiny portion of the machine could be seen.

He began to teach me. His father, Tom, owned an old Allis-Chalmers B, and I was invited to come over for a demonstration, a test ride, and my first opportunity to cut a field on a real tractor. To say that I was unhitched would be an understatement. It was one of those sudden and total fascinations that I preferred not to have explained to me. I only wanted to savor it. I wanted a tractor of my own, though I had no reason, no farm, to justify such an acquisition.

David and I, sometimes his dad and one or two of the other kids, would set out after school now and then, to visit a dealer or a farm. There were long, long conversations about the merits and failings of

Famous Ford

Ford's famous N Series made its debut with the 9N in 1939, followed by the 2N in 1942, and the 8N in 1948, although 8N production actually began in mid-1947. This 1948 8N was remanufactured by N-Complete. (Photograph by Andrew Morland)

this or that as we aired our curiosities. There were more opportunities to drive. On my desk, a small collection of sales literature and farm magazines germinated. My vocabulary and my focus about tractors began to resolve. Had I become rehitched?

One day, an acquaintance called from one of the horse farms. He knew of a tractor that had been in a fire several months before, and it had been towed out to the junk pile to decompose. David and I went right over to see it. He identified it as a Ford 8N with a lift system originally designed by Harry Ferguson. He began to describe each lever and function.

We decided that the fire burned intensely hot, but briefly—a gas tank leak, probably. All rubber, composition, or light metal had burned or melted, but in its haste to pass, the fire had left the inner machine intact. It might run again, this 8N, although the completely rusted remains tried to conceal this secret. We were excited about the challenge, and David promised to help.

I offered to buy it. The man said, "Take it." We rushed to David's house to borrow the front wheels from the Allis-Chalmers B, then back to our heap to mount them. We towed it out of the junk and into the field. The seals looked good. Each move was a gesture of promise.

We waited for late evening to minimize encounters with traffic, then towed that tractor twenty-eight miles back to my house. Our excitement would not subside, although it was now past midnight. We just had to put it on blocks . . . just begin some disassembly . . . just the front grille . . . just the old burnt wires . . . just this . . . just that. . . .

Before long we had removed enough parts that we needed to establish an order for storing them, and make some notes for the resplendent days of reassembly that were ahead. Until then, we would take apart all but the inner engine and transmission.

The next day, we got some cardboard boxes to organize the parts removal and went off to the Ford dealer to look at parts books and service manuals. We mapped out a plan for what had to be replaced or rebuilt. Would it be easy to get parts for a then twenty-year-old tractor?

No problem! In David's file cabinet were the names and numbers of used parts dealers all over the country. Instead, in our next visit to our dealer, we told him of our project, and I offered to buy the parts from him if he would coach us through the difficult tasks.

Again, no problem! Many old tractors are well-supported with replacements, unlike car parts, which become exhausting to locate once a vehicle becomes ten to fifteen years old. Today, although some of the 9Ns are nearly sixty years old, Ford—now New Holland—supports more than 90 percent available parts replacement.

Restoring an old tractor or implement is more a matter of attitude than task. The hours passed during take-down, wire brushing, repainting, and rebuilding are a vague entity hidden by the absorbing enjoyment of deciding to do it and measuring the progress. It is possible to sense the engineering integrity.

In reassembly there is a strength greater than new, it seems. But my favorite discovery was quite unexpected. When I had begun to operate my 8N six months later, I was certain I could feel every single part that I had touched, working in an aggregate unity and separately as well.

The drawings in the manuals, the connections of all the parts to each other, their entire articulation, had become a tactile reality. I felt it in the steering, at the clutch, in the seat under me, and in the sounds and smells. Since then, and over these many years, I have known exactly and immediately which part was feeling a strain, which part would need service. Every operator should have to restore a machine to improve operating skills and senses. One then operates in such a way to deliberately protect each part.

Ford heritage
FACING PAGE, TOP: *The Ford 801 Powermaster of 1957–1961 continued the heritage of the N Series tractors that were launched in 1939. This 1959 801 was remanufactured by N-Complete. Owner: Lester Neal of Seymour, Indiana. (Photograph by Andrew Morland)*

Hot-rod tractor
FACING PAGE, BOTTOM: *Twins Howard and Joe Funk of Coffeyville, Kansas, offered kits to convert Ford tractors to use Ford straight six-cylinder and V-8 engines from automobiles and trucks. The result was a hot-rodded farm tractor unlike anything else plowing a field in the 1940s and 1950s. This V-8–powered 1952 8N features dual chromed exhaust stacks. Owner: Robert Meyer of Gurnee, Illinois. (Photograph by Andrew Morland)*

I had no uses for my 8N, though. No farm, no big tract of land. My family and neighbors all wondered what I would do with it. It was enough for me just to have it, to like it, and to drive it around. I felt a pride in bringing it back to life, and the tractor itself was living proof.

One day, I received an invitation to drive it in a 4th of July parade. I had been giving the kids rides in the trailer, so why not? Then, more serious ideas began to occur. The old Wagner loader was a perfect tool for lifting bundles of shingles up to the roof, saving my energy for the roofing job itself. Then, a stone wall was needed to enhance the landscaping. What a backsaver, that 8N! When I realized I could actually dig for the foundation of a new carport myself, it was thrilling. I could bring in the firewood! I could help a neighbor whose car was stuck in the mud. It was easy to fell a tree in a specific direction. And so, my lifelong dependence had begun.

One day I recognized that my tractor knew how to help itself. A rear tire had gone flat. It was filled with calcium solution and impossibly heavy for me. I blocked the axle, removed the tire, and carefully, so it wouldn't fall, rolled it forward to chain it to the loader. Then I lifted it into the air and backed my pickup under it, lowered it, and went to the repair place. When I returned, I reversed the operation. Simple!

My son and nephews all learned to drive it from about age eight. As high schoolers, they put it to use in their summertime business to earn college expenses. We found a York rake and took jobs building driveways, parking areas, and lawns. The boys even enjoyed giving the 8N another cleaning and repainting.

Then I bought another tractor, a 2N, with a better loader, intending to refurbish both and to switch the better loader to my 8N. Both tractor and loader were badly rusted and had some worn parts, but they've been restored also. In fact, I've now restored four tractors, three loaders, a flail knife mower, a York rake, a spreader, a snow blower, two rear blades, and a trailer. The task has become so easy because it is so rewarding.

Today, I can't imagine how I might have done without my fabulous Ford 8N. Teasingly, my family tells

SINGING THE FORDSON'S PRAISE
Anonymous, 1910s

The Fordson on the farm arose
Before the dawn at four:
It milked the cows and washed the clothes
And finished every chore.

Then forth it went into the field
Just at the break of day,
It reaped and threshed the golden yield
And hauled it all away.

It plowed the field that afternoon,
And when the job was through
It hummed a pleasant little tune
And churned the butter, too.

For while the farmer, peaceful-eyed,
Read by the tungsten's glow,
His patient Fordson stood outside
And ran the dynamo.

everyone that I won't even think about going on vacation unless I can bring the 8N.

I was so excited about it that I began to publish the 9N-2N-8N *Newsletter*, a homespun quarterly intended for N-nuts like me. We are mesmerized by the spirit of these great old tractors, and devoted to preserving them and their history.

These old Fords are so evenly tempered, so forgiving in use, so simple to knock down in a few strokes, that even a novice can change a part. They are so practical to own and use, and so efficient at doing what they were designed to do, and so subtly beautiful in their Art Deco motif, and so inspiring to a pride of ownership, and so refreshingly unlike so many of the throwaway things of today.

Now, as my subscribers from all over the country exchange their questions and answers, and tell their N-stories, I learn new things nearly every day. My 8N has been like a school or a special door opening to experiences, pleasures, and associations I never imagined I could have.

Ferguson expertise

Irish renegade inventor Harry Ferguson was instrumental in developing the three-point hitch and other components of the Ferguson System for the Ford 9N and 2N tractors. When Ferguson had a falling out with Ford, he started building his own Ferguson tractors, which were often as good, if not better, than the Ford machines of the era. Ferguson joined forces in 1953 with the Canadian giant, Massey-Harris to create the great Massey-Ferguson firm that is today among the world's dominant agricultural machinery manufacturers. This 1955 Ferguson TEF-20 diesel is owned by Brian Whitlock, Yoevil, Great Britain. (Photograph by Andrew Morland)

Duck Soup

By Bill Vossler

Bill Vossler deserves the title "tractor detective" for his extraordinary book, *Orphan Tractors*. His sleuthing to uncover the history of the lost tractor makes—from Avery to Rumely, Happy Farmer to Waterloo Boy—has created a masterful collection of tractor lore. Bill is also a historian of toy tractors and regularly writes for *Toy Farmer* magazine.

In this story, Bill tells of a harrowing incident in his youth, when he learned to drive a tractor, outran a prairie storm, and learned a bit more about himself as a person.

During summers on the North Dakota prairie, we were often forewarned of bad weather because we could see it pile up far off on the horizon, sometimes early in the day, through wavy sheets of heat. And so most farmers in those days kept one eye cocked toward the horizon with a mind as to what the weather might allow them to do—or not to do—that workday.

But Gordie, the farmer I worked for, was no ordinary farmer. He owned a gift of gab, as well as the local sales barn (which, rumor had it, he had won in a high-stakes poker game in the back room of a local bar), and farming wasn't his highest priority. This was why he needed a hired hand, and eventually I filled that bill between my junior and senior years of high school. I had just turned seventeen.

Unfortunately, I was no normal hired hand. I knew as much about agriculture as you might expect from a farming-area city kid who had picked rock, hauled bales, and once or twice butchered chickens and pigs. This might not have been a problem, except that Gordie was seldom around to help me or direct me or give me advice.

On that fateful morning, Gordie had already hopped into his pickup and was hightailing it out of the yard ahead of a plume of dust when I flagged him down and asked him what he wanted me to do.

"Oh yeah," he said, removing his co-op hat and scratching his white scalp. "Well, why don't you take the B and the hayrack and load them bales from that field I showed you yesterday? That should do you most of the day." He glanced at the sky. "Might rain," he said, and then he floored it and was gone, hidden in a cloud of dust before I could yell that I'd not only never driven the Allis-Chalmers B before, but I'd never driven a tractor before. And I'd only driven a car once or twice.

If you were a steady and dependable kid, the people in my small town would assume that you could handle pretty much anything, which is why I routinely collected bills for Sayler Bros. Hardware, pedaling around town with a couple thousand in cash stuffed in my back pocket every month, ran the projector at the Dakota Theatre five nights a week, and delivered all the newspapers in town.

And that was why Gordie figured I could handle a tractor without too much trouble—which proved to be true, at least at the outset. Soon I was proudly standing on the tractor platform getting a feeling for the steering as the little beast bounced over the prairie roads toward my date with destiny, trailing a clattering flatbed hayrack behind. Duck soup, I figured, as I spotted a pair of tractor-sized boulders—you

Driving tractor

An Amish girl keeps a careful eye on her direction as her Deere tractor pulls a New Holland baler and a hay wagon. (Photograph by Jerry Irwin)

wouldn't want to crash into them with a vehicle—that signaled the entrance to a steep, sloping path choked with stinkweed. I negotiated the narrow way between the boulders to the nearly invisible path, and nearly killed the little tractor before I goosed the Allis B up the long steep hill on top of which storm clouds seemed to be piling.

But the day was young, the clouds far away, and I was weaving the lies I would tell my friends about what size tractor Gordie had let me drive my second day at work—maybe a brand-new 5010 John Deere that had just come out, and the factory had asked him to test (he'd tested several products prior to their coming onto the market, although no tractors) or a Minneapolis Moline G-VI. I certainly didn't want to tell my friends that the first tractor I'd ever driven was a dinky little Allis B, and this was definitely a dinky one. It was the first Allis B of late-1930s vintage, and seemed not much bigger than a go-cart to a kid who wanted to drive a big tractor. My friends would make fun of me all winter if they ever found out.

The air was soupy, and the sweat bees swarmed and bumped into my bare back as I pulled off into an alfalfa field. At first I wasn't sure it was the right field, but then I saw the bales. They were small and square because Gordie was too busy to adjust his baler. He said they were the perfect size for one person to haul.

That was true, I discovered as I idled the B beside a group of bales, tossed them onto the hayrack, climbed up, and hoisted them to their proper positions on the rack, and then drove on to the next group. I felt like a real farmer.

I filled the bottom row, and then most of the second, third, and fourth rows, leaving an area to toss the bales, and a path for me to climb up the rows. Time flew by. Clouds had blotted out the sun long before, and a cool breeze had thankfully sprung up. I had nearly filled all the rows when I paused for a minute to glance at the sky. Instead of puffy clouds or long gentle white ones, the sky had turned variously gun-metal gray, angry black, and purple as a bruised grape.

While I had worked, the anvil-topped black clouds had clawed miles up into the atmosphere, until now they towered menacingly over me, their hulking weight pressing down ominously, dwarfing the hayrack and the Allis and me. All I could say was, "Uh oh." I felt alone and tiny and insignificant.

A white zigzag of lightning sizzled across the sky, followed instantly by a clap of thunder that nearly startled me off the edge of the hayrack. I tried to calmly finish pushing the last bales of the load into their slots as a cold wind surged and the first fat raindrops plopped in the dust and plinked on the Allis.

I scrambled down, climbed onto the cabless tractor, and slowly turned it around, puttering toward the prairie path and home. I knew I was in for a little blow. Had I been wiser or more experienced, I would simply have crawled under the hayrack and waited for it to pass. But Gordie had said something about not wanting those bales to get wet, and, well, I simply didn't know what I was doing.

A hundred yards of driving and the deluge from the skies opened, drenching me instantly in ice-cold rain, and blotting out the landscape around me. I could have been in a blizzard, for all I could see. I was all alone with the gray hissing rain, howling wind, and crackling thunder. I trembled at every flash and noise, and when the hail began pummeling me, I shoved the Allis into high, and decided to outrun the storm.

For a few moments, it was actually fun. To control my terror, I whooped and yelled as though I was on an old-time cattle drive trying to keep the beasts together during the storm. Had anyone seen me, my white-knuckled hands knotted around the steering wheel, black hair streaming behind, teeth gritted, and a maniacal look in my eyes as the rain cascaded around me and pellets of snow-white hail bounced off the hood of the orange Allis, they would have thought me insane. If you have ever been caught unprotected in the open during a prairie storm, you'll know that I probably was, a little bit.

Finally, with whips of white lightning and growls of thunder reverberating around me, I came to my senses. Ozone burned my nostrils as I bounced along the path. I peered behind me into the stinging rain and saw that bales were beginning to jar loose.

But before I could slow, the earth seemed to give way. The front edge of the tractor, the back wheels,

Corn harvest
A Case DC general-purpose tractor pulls a corn harvester on the farm of Fremont Crouch of Hoopeston, Illinois, in the 1940s. (Photograph by J. C. Allen and Son)

RAMBLINGS AT THE THRESHERMEN'S REUNION

By Ed Klimuska of Lancaster County, Pennsylvania

This is a Geiser steam engine from Waynesboro, Pennsylvania," says Jim Martin, who was having a great time running the huge contraption.

Martin lives in Gap, Pennsylvania. He works in a bank. But once a year, at the threshermen's reunion, he enjoys putting on old clothes, getting dirty, and running a steam engine like the 1903 Geiser, which is owned by a friend.

"I always operate someone else's engine," he says. "This is a vacation for me. Instead of hunting or fishing over the year, I'm taking my time off now. I'm spending my vacation here."

The smoke is billowing. The engine is chugging and coughing. And Martin is inching along very, very slow.

Martin was operating a steam engine that was providing power for shingle making. The old steam engines provided power for many jobs, just not farm chores.

"It's fun being around these guys who used these steam engines every day for a living. For them, it started as just a remembrance. They just remember the old days, how to fire one of these things up and all the trouble it was to get the farm work done."

Well-earned rest
With a bird resting on its exhaust stack, a Deere 4010 Diesel sits on the edge of a hayfield in Medina, North Dakota. (Photograph by Paul Rezendes)

Machinery hill
Looking dapper in their fair-going best, farm folk examine with a well-trained eye the latest machinery offering from Oliver at the 1934 Minnesota State Fair's Machinery Hill. (Minnesota Historical Society collection)

and suddenly the entire hayrack was slanting downward and gaining speed. The hill!

I'd forgotten about that long and steep hill I'd climbed up to get to the alfalfa field. There was one other little knell of warning in my brain, but before I could capture it, my attention was pulled back to the tractor.

I was going too fast. I had to slow down. Bales had begun to bounce off the side of the hayrack, disappearing into the torrents of rain and hail. I shoved in the clutch, and tried to downshift. But it wouldn't slip into another gear. Now I was in neutral, and if I had not already been sopping wet, I would have been covered in sweat, because I knew I was in big trouble. The unfettered tractor and hayrack and I picked up amazing speed, plunging wildly down the hill, clanging and clattering and crashing into dips and ruts in the road. I was tossed every which way. My teeth ached from the jarring. Fenceposts were a blur. Bales shot

by me on both sides, ejected from the rack. Half the time I was in the air, tethered to the machine only by my death grip on the steering wheel.

I had to stop. So I jammed on the brakes. The rear wheels of the Allis locked, and began skidding. I glanced behind me, and the hairs on the nape of my neck prickled. The hayrack had turned almost sideways, and was skidding recklessly towards me, the hitch bent at a "V" where it was attached to the Allis. I felt the front wheels of the Allis lift off the ground. Half the bales were gone, and the others were jouncing around in the rack, seeking an exit.

Lightning smashed into the field not a dozen feet away. The clap of thunder was deafening. The tractor skidded sideways, front wheels in the air like a rearing pony, back wheels gouging out great gouts of wet black dirt and spewing it off to the side.

Then I remembered what my subconscious had been trying to warn me about: the boulders at the

Orchard worker

Tractors designed for working orchards developed to include cowling over the wheels and cockpit so the machines would not snag and damage precious tree limbs. This 1941 McCormick-Deering O-4 orchard model looks almost like a racing car—or race tractor—due to its nearly streamlined appearance. Owners: the Steward brothers of Springport, Michigan. (Photograph by Ralph W. Sanders)

THE FARMALL REVOLUTIONIZES FARMING
By F. P. LeCompte of Virginia, 1929

I considered my Farmall the most wonderful tractor made. I cultivated, mowed hay, plowed, disked, ran our binder, cut wood, etc. I was astonished at the amount and kinds of work it did. The Farmall was to my mind the greatest piece of machinery ever brought to the farm. I could not praise the Farmall too highly. I really loved to use it.

Family farm
Nestled in the rolling hills of East Albany, Vermont, this farm, with its classic red barn, basks in the sunshine. (Photograph by Jerry Irwin)

entryway to the road I was now careening down. In my mind's eye I could see the tractor piling up against one of the boulders, followed by the hayrack slamming into it, pulverizing the little Allis and me.

I could feel the force of the hayrack behind me, controlling me, and instinctively I knew that in seconds the drama would be over: I would soon tip over, or be tossed off and ground under, or smashed into the rock.

So I did the only thing I could do: I released the brakes. For a moment the small tractor and hayrack and I continued sliding sideways down the hill to-

ward the rocks. Then slowly the rear tractor wheels gained purchase, the front end touched earth, and the tractor found the road. In short order, the hayrack followed as though nothing untoward had happened.

There was but one thing to do now, and I did it. I grasped the steering wheel, gritted my teeth, and rode the clattering beast down the rest of the hill. Now I knew how Pecos Bill of myth felt when he rode a tornado. With breathtaking speed, the huge boulders loomed up out of the mist, and then I shot the gap between them—one wheel of the hayrack scraping past—and I darted across the main road (if another

Descendant of a long history

ABOVE: *Oliver had a long, proud tradition of building farm equipment—first with its famous chilled plow, and later with a full range of tractors and implements. The Oliver 660 took over from the 66 and was built from 1959 through 1964. This 660 is owned by the Antique Gas & Steam Engine Museum in Vista, California. (Photograph by Vincent Manocchi)*

Out to pasture

LEFT: *A tree grows through the remains of a Deere tractor put out to pasture. (Photograph by Andy Kraushaar)*

vehicle had been coming, I would have been in pieces small enough for soup, for sure). I drove onto another grassy road on the other side. I bounced and jounced and rattled, until with judicious use of the brakes, I calmed the beast down, slowed it, and stopped.

And there I sat, trembling, sucking air, and blowing as hard as a horse that had been ill-used, while the wind roared and the rain washed over my face and the occasional hailstone rapped me on the head. I just sat while lightning crackled overhead and thunder boomed, until I stopped shaking.

Shortly, the worst of the storm blew over. I turned the tractor around and slowly headed between the rocks and back up the hill. Only a few bales remained in the rack. The rest were strewn up and down the hill, and on either side, like casualties of a great war.

The storm clouds blew away, the sun peeped out, and I began picking up the bales and carting them back to the hayrack one by one, until I had it filled.

At supper, Gordie smiled mischievously and asked how my first tractor ride had gone.

"Um, pretty good," I lied. "Except the storm slowed me down a little bit."

"What about that hill? Any trouble?"

"Not really," I lied again. "A little tricky, maybe."

"Good, good," he said. "I came home that way, and saw that somebody else had some trouble on that hill," he said, "judging by how the road was tore up."

I inhaled some soup into the wrong pipe, and spluttered and coughed for a while. When I regained my voice I said, "That is a tricky hill. But other than that, my first day on a tractor was duck soup."

Resting in peace

After a long life of labor, a United tractor rests in peace on the edge of a farm field. If this tractor bears a close resemblance to an Allis-Chalmers, it is no mistake. United Tractor & Equipment Company of Chicago, Illinois, contracted in 1929 with Allis to construct the United tractor, but when the United venture folded, Allis added the tractor to its line and renamed it the Model U. Over the years, many firms bought contract-built tractors and relabeled them; a classic case is that of the Illinois Tractor Company of Bloomington, Illinois, and the Robert Bell Engine & Thresher Company of Seaforth, Ontario, where the American-market Illinois Super-Drive was imported into Canada as Bell's Imperial Super-Drive. (Photograph by Andy Kraushaar)

Minneapolis-Moline tractors, then . . .
LEFT: *The showroom of the Seidel Implement Company in Rallinger, Texas, featured a heady display of the latest in Minneapolis-Moline wares, including the Universal Model Z tractor. The poster above the office highlights two World War II documentaries, "In Our Own American Way" along with "Thunder Heads Over The Pacific," sponsored by Minne-Mo. (Minnesota Historical Society collection)*

. . . Minneapolis-Moline tractors, now
BELOW: *Featuring its novel enclosed cab and road gears, Minne-Mo's 1938–1941 UDLX Comfortractor was new, radical, a vision of the future of farm tractors—and a sales failure. Only some 125 were ever built; today they are one of the ultimate tractor collectibles. (Photograph by Jerry Irwin)*

Chapter 5

A Living History

"You can't be involved with ageless iron very long before you find yourself learning things you would never have suspected in your wildest dreams you would pick up while pounding on stuck pistons or prying at rusted bolts—history, agriculture, geography, economics, dancing, dressing a bleeding artery, the intricacies of filing for bankruptcy, and where to find a good marriage counselor, for example."
—Roger Welsch

Vintage farm tractors may be ancient and obsolete, but through the hard work and busted knuckles of tractor restorers, history lives on. Threshing bees, tractor shows, and farming museums keep our agricultural past alive for future generations, illuminating the blood, sweat, and tears that built the family farm.

These essays are moving, loving, and even humorous looks at the tractor collector's and restorer's art.

Parade of power
LARGE PHOTO: *A ribbon of Farmall Red: International Harvester tractors join the Parade of Power at the Rough and Tumble Thresherman's Reunion in Lancaster County, Pennsylvania. (Photograph by Jerry Irwin)*

Tractor lineup
INSET: *After the 1929 merger that formed Minneapolis-Moline Company, a decal was added to the side of the Twin City tractor from Minneapolis Steel & Machinery Company to mark it as a Minne-Mo product. These tractors were lined up outside the firm's factory on Lake Street in Minneapolis. (Minnesota Historical Society collection)*

A Life-Changing Experience

By Robert N. Pripps

Bob Pripps was born in 1932 on a small farm in northern Wisconsin, and developed an infatuation with things mechanical at an early age. Through the years, he worked with many different makes and models of tractors and crawlers, and earned his private pilot's license by the time he graduated from high school. Bob became a flight test engineer on the RF-101 Voodoo, and later worked on Atlas missile base activation for General Dynamics and jet engine starter and constant speed drive testing for the Sundstrand Corporation. But through all of his mechanical interests, he has remained faithful to tractors.

After retiring, Bob began writing a book on his favorite tractor, the Ford. The book was published in 1990, teaming Bob with renowned English automotive photographer Andrew Morland. Since then, Bob and Andrew have collaborated on eleven books on classic tractors, including his latest, *Vintage Ford Tractors*, published by Voyageur Press. Bob has also authored five other tractor titles on his own.

This essay serves as a memoir of Bob's infatuation with tractors.

When I was fourteen years old, I had a life-changing experience. The father of my best friend, Earl Hedberg, obtained the first Ford-Ferguson tractor in the area. Abject envy is not a pretty thing, but that's what happened. It was in no way sated until I got my own 2N at age fifty.

My earliest tractor experience, however, came at about age six. My maternal grandfather was a farmer in northcentral Wisconsin. It was, I believe, a McCormick 10-20 that he was using to pull a spiked toothed drag. Grandpa heisted me aboard, to ride hanging onto the fender. Hang on I did, for dear life,

for speed seemed to be of the essence. I was plenty glad when the ride was over.

At age nine, I had my first tractor driving experience. My dad, a Wisconsin Conservation Department Forest Ranger, was disking a fire lane, with me along for the ride. The tractor was an Allis-Chalmers crawler, probably a Model M. I suppose Dad got bored plodding up and down the lane and offered me the controls. I did not relinquish them until we ran out of gas late in the day.

When I was growing up, kids that didn't live on farms—like me—hired themselves out to work on farms. During the summer of 1944 when I was twelve, I worked on the Wyandotte Farm for Ed Teufert. Ed was one of the lucky few farmers who was able to buy

Starting young

A life-changing experience: A youngster examines the latest offering from Deere at the Minnesota State Fair in the 1950s. (Minnesota State Fair collection)

a brand-new tractor during those war years. What he got was a shiny red Farmall H. Since I was still pretty small to do the heavy farm work, I got to do most of the driving of the H.

My curiosity with things mechanical almost cost me my life at age twelve. That November (it was Thanksgiving vacation from school), Ed Teufert was having trouble starting his '41 Dodge truck, due to the extreme northern Wisconsin cold. I went out to give him a hand, dressing myself in several layers of sweaters and a wool coat. Using the Farmall for a pull, we soon had the Dodge running. Now I, having nothing more interesting to do, began fooling around with an old Gallion road grader that had been left idling in our yard. The grader operator had gotten cold plowing snow and had walked home for some hot coffee. Soon, my mitten got caught around the power take-off shaft, and I was lifted up off the ground as my arm wrapped around the shaft. The Gallion's engine chugged its last, just as my arm was stretched to its limit. Rescuers later said I was saved from losing my arm by all the layers of clothing I had on. Regarding my right thumb, however, I was not so lucky. The last chug pulled off my leather mitten with my thumb still inside.

Through my high school years, my tractor experience was focused on crawlers owned by the state of Wisconsin. My first summer after high school graduation, I worked for the Forests and Parks Division, gaining experience with several more Allis-Chalmers crawlers and bulldozers.

For several decades, I led what might be called a tractor-free existence. But along the way, I inherited thirty acres of maple forest that were part of the Wisconsin farm on which I was born. On this land, I started harvesting sap for maple syrup, and soon needed the help of mechanical horsepower.

It was not until I was fifty that I finally was able to purchase the tractor of my youthful infatuation: the Ford-Ferguson of my friend's dad. My own budding maple syrup operation finally "justified" the purchase of a 1946 Ford-Ferguson 2N.

Since then, a 1948 John Deere B and a John Deere 440C bulldozer (since sold) were added and have appeared in many of my books on antique and collectible tractors.

Dreams
Generations of farmers and tractors come together in Bob Artley's evocative cartoon from his series "Memories of a Former Kid."

Deere tractors, then . . .
ABOVE: *A 1935 Deere Model B tractor pulls a No. 10 Deere corn picker near Dell Rapids, South Dakota. (Deere & Company archives)*

. . . Deere tractors, now
LEFT: *A stunning 1933 Deere GPWT. Owner: Verlan Heberer of Belleville, Illinois. (Photograph by Ralph W. Sanders)*

BITTEN BY THE FORDSON BUG
By Duane Helman of Rosewood, Ohio

I was raised on a farm, but we never had a Fordson. Dad used a 10/20 McCormick and a 2N Ford-Ferguson. In later years, when I was out on my own, I began to collect and restore classic cars. Soon this hobby became too expensive for me to enjoy, so I picked up a Fordson and restored it. Since then, Fordsons have become an avocation. I have owned lots of them, including a rare X Model used by Henry Ford & Son in developing the Fordson. Now, among others, my collection boasts of fifty 1938 model Fordson tractors.

"Fordsicle"
Covered in ice and icicles, a trusty Ford 8N waits for its owner in Royalston, Massachusetts. (Photograph by Paul Rezendes)

Minneapolis-Moline tractors, then . . .

Half family car, half family farm tractor, this Minneapolis-Moline UDLX Comfortractor was used to drop the children at school before heading off to work the fields as depicted in this Minne-Mo advertising photograph from the firm's archives. M-M expected the tractor-cum-car concept to be ideal for rural farm families in the United States and Canada who needed a tractor but could not afford a separate car. (Minnesota Historical Society collection)

FERGUSON TE-20 THRIVES ON NEGLECT
By Bryan Laurence of England

I found my Fergie in a peat bog. It had been there for a couple of years when I found it. We pulled it out and the engine started on the second swing. We took a bucket of peat out of the gearbox, but otherwise, it was not in bad condition. Within ten months, it was totally restored.

. . . Minneapolis-Moline tractors, now

A beautifully restored 1938 UDLX parked in front of a classic round barn. Owner: Donald Kingen of McCordsville, Indiana. (Photograph by Ralph W. Sanders)

The Saga of the Farmall 400

By Claire D. Scheibe

Claire Scheibe is well known to toy tractor collectors around the globe. As publisher of *Toy Farmer* magazine, he has been influential in developing and shaping the hobby.

Claire was farming the Scheibe family farm near LaMoure, North Dakota, when *Toy Farmer* had its genesis. He always had an interest in tractor toys and antiques, and began buying and selling the toys, turning a hobby into a business. Buying up a batch of obsolete toys from the famous Ertl Company, including Cockshutt and Oliver tractors, as well as New Holland implements, Claire started mailing out a single-page typewritten letter to other budding collectors. This newsletter evolved into *Toy Farmer*, which is read and studied by toy tractor collectors everywhere.

But in the beginning, it was naturally the real McCoy that inspired Claire—his father's International Harvester. In this essay, he writes of the family farm's IH, and how he tracked down a similar tractor to restore as part of his family's heritage.

From the earliest time I can remember, my dad was an IH guy. Dad started farming in 1939 with a team of already worn and tired horses, and it didn't taken him long to realize that he needed mechanical horsepower. He scouted up a Farmall F-12, which served as our main power source on our 160 acres throughout World War II. I might add that lugs on the F-12 were replaced with strip rubber that provided my dad with a mark of luxury in our community.

After the war was over, my dad once again went in search of even more horsepower. He found a barely used International M, a John Deere field cultivator, a four-row corn cultivator, and an almost-new, four-bottom sixteenth plow, all for the grand total price of $1,000. We were then on our way through International Harvester Hs, a 400, a 450, and a 650 before we switched to Allis-Chalmers, and later, John Deere.

Through the years, I've thought about the many different tractors we've had and their importance to me personally. I have always had a special place in my heart for that streamlined beauty, the Farmall 400. It was a real favorite, because I started farming with this tractor in 1958. I remember how easy it was to handle. It was also my first experience with the Torque Converter, which was used at times in our farming operation as an "overdrive." It was with pride that you drove that Farmall 400, pulling four bottoms and a pony-press at a record-breaking speed of more than four miles per hour. It gave you a great feeling! At the

Farmland

White barns and farmhouses stand out amidst the wavy patterns of cultivated fields of Pennsylvania farmland. (Photograph by Jerry Irwin)

time, we farmed more than 1,000 acres, and the Farmall proved that a real deep admiration could develop between operator and machine. As time passed, the Farmall 400 went in on trade for a Farmall 450 diesel, which had more power and many of the familiar features.

Several years passed, and I became serious about finding a restorable Farmall 400. The search finally ended at a rural farm outside Emerado, North Dakota. A farmer who was in his later years of farming said he had bought the "old girl" when they were last for sale. He said the 400 was used for only a couple of seasons before he purchased an IH 560. The Farmall 400 was then put in a shed for "future use."

It was my fortune that the "future use" would come from me. I ended up purchasing and moving the 400 to my home in LaMoure, North Dakota, where that "old girl" would be restored and put on display as part of the Toy Farmer Museum properties.

The Hazards of Tractor Collecting
By Lynn Pollesch

The Brothers Pollesch own about fifteen or so nicely restored Oliver and Cletrac tractors. When asked if their wives objected to the growing collection, Lynn said, "Oh, we take new additions over to Dad's place for a while."

Hometown tractor

International Harvester and Chicago, Illinois, shared a long history. In the center background of this photograph stands the Equitable Building, which occupies two of the three lots on which Cyrus Hall McCormick's Reaper Works was originally built. IH was later headquartered in the Equitable Building for decades. Chicago's WGN radio farm broadcaster and personality Max Armstrong proudly poses with his restored 1953 Farmall Super H. (Photograph by Ralph W. Sanders)

The toy . . .

ABOVE: *Miniature tractors have found homes in the collections of toy farmers everywhere. This Canadian Massey-Harris 555 is a die-cast miniature made by the famed Ertl Company of Dyersville, Iowa. (Photograph by Andy Kraushaar)*

. . . And the real McCoy

LEFT: *A stylish Canadian-made 1938 Massey-Harris 101 Twin-Power. Owner: Richard Prince of Conover, Ohio. (Photograph by Ralph W. Sanders)*

RAMBLINGS AT THE
THRESHERMEN'S REUNION
By Ed Klimuska of Lancaster County, Pennsylvania

Floyd Thompson lives in Unionville, Pennsylvania. He's retired from a nonfarm job, and farms a few acres.

He has an interest in old John Deere tractors. One of his best finds was a 1946 LA model that was a one-plow tractor, the smallest tractor the company produced at the time.

His son, who lives in Connecticut, saw the tractor in a nearby lawn. "I went clear up there to get it in 1992," Thompson says. "I had to make a special trip."

Thompson says the tractor, being strictly for small farms, took the place of horses.

Thompson was thrilled with his find. It had all the attachments: the plow, the cultivator, the muller, and wheel weights. "It's rare to find so much apparatus with a tractor," Thompson says. "I really have the whole complement."

Roger's Rules for Collecting Old Iron and Living with Your Wife

By Roger Welsch

Roger Welsch needs little introduction, especially to vintage tractor fans. As a television personality on the CBS *Sunday Morning* program, Roger has spread the word about rural life wherever the airwaves travel. His writings on tractors appear regularly in *Successful Farming* magazine's "Ageless Iron" section, as well as in *Esquire*, *Smithsonian*, and *Nebraska Farmer*. In addition, he is the author of more than twenty books, including *Old Tractors and the Men Who Love Them* and *Busted Tractors and Rusty Knuckles*. As John Carter of the Nebraska State Historical Society noted, "We all knew sooner or later that Roger would write a book about religion."

In this article with its wise philosophy, Roger explains his rules on how to keep your tractors happy and your family running.

There's more to collecting and restoring old tractors than nuts and bolts. A lot more. Nuts and bolts are the least of it.

Don't get me wrong: Lovely Linda is a wonderful wife and friend and has endured more than any one woman should have to. I'm the first to admit that life with me isn't easy. I admit that, even though I don't always believe it.

Things got tense when I began collecting Allis-Chalmers WC tractors. I had one WC for almost 20 years before it occurred to me that it might be nice to have two. And once I had two, I thought it would really be handy to have a couple of WCs around for parts, but along with the parts tractors I got a couple of "runners." So then there were six. And I got a good deal on one that had been sitting in a shed for nearly 25 years, and I have another couple lined up not far from here.

If you're married and are thinking about getting into the old iron business, forget trivial things like socket wrenches and bearing pullers and lay the groundwork for your new hobby by carefully studying the following rules:

Rule 1: Collect only one model and make of tractor—nothing but John Deere Bs or Allis-Chalmers Gs, for example. When all your tractors are the same color and shape, it's harder, if not impossible, for anyone (if you catch my drift) to figure out how many tractors you actually have.

Rule 2: Never line up your tractors, ever. Nothing

How long you been driving tractor?
A youngster pilots his Massey-Ferguson 390 pedal tractor, pulling a miniature utility wagon carrying his younger brother. (Photograph by Jerry Irwin)

distresses a difficult spouse more than seeing twelve old tractors lined up, looking for all the world like a burning pile of hundred dollar bills. Scatter the tractors around—a couple behind the shed, one or two in the shed, another beside the garage—so that it is not possible for anyone (if you know who I mean) to see more than two or three from any one perspective. Your hobby will be less "irritating" that way.

Rule 3: For pretty much the same reason, don't number your tractors. Give them names. You'd be surprised how much less trouble you will have if you talk about "Sweet Allis" rather than "Allis Chalmers WC No. 14."

Rule 4: Early in your collecting, buy a tractor you don't want. Sell it as quickly as you can. Don't worry about making money on the transaction. The main thing is to get a tractor and get rid of it. Then you can say, "Yes, Angel-face, I do have six Deere Bs, and they are in the shed while our car is out in the weather. That doesn't mean I will always have six Deere Bs. *Remember the one I got rid of? I'm thinking of selling another one any day now so we can put the car in the garage.*" If you have a friend who collects tractors, make arrangements for him to drop off a tractor now and again. That way you can say—if anyone asks—that you bought it. Then have it hauled off again, and say you sold it. With this system, you reestablish your reputation for moderation.

Warning: About the time I accumulated my sixth or seventh Allis WC I bought a lovely little Allis C. Linda and our 9-year-old daughter Antonia were in the farmyard as I unloaded this lovely little item. "I see you bought yourself another tractor that doesn't run," said Linda.

"Guess what, dear?" I beamed. "I didn't buy myself another Allis. I bought you an Allis! She's yours, and ain't she cute?" I wasn't at all prepared for what she said next.

"How much can I get for it?"

"Er, uh, I didn't get it for you to sell, honey-cakes. I was thinking, if you don't want to drive it all the time, I can take it into town now and then just to keep the oil stirred up for you. It won't be any trouble at all."

"Well, thanks, Rog, you're really too sweet. I don't deserve a darling like you. How much can I get for it?"

I almost broke into tears at the thought of some-

one loading that tractor and driving off with it. But, about that time my mind kicked into road gear. "Actually, I thought that if you wouldn't mind sharing, it could be Antonia's tractor. Right. That's it! Eventually it'll be Antonia's tractor."

Antonia leaped into the C's seat with a squeal and started twisting the steering wheel and making tractor noises. Linda snorted something about me fixing my own supper and headed back toward the house while I helped Antonia bond with her tractor. That was a close call, and my advice to you is not to buy your wife a tractor.

Rule 5: Pay for tractors with a cashier's check, postal money order, or cash, which leaves far less evidence than checks drawn on the family account. Once you have gotten possession of a tractor and paid for it, *eat the stubs, carbon copies, or receipts immediately.* Such things have a way of becoming an embarrassment later, take it from me.

Rule 6: Now and then buy a wreck "for parts," even if you don't need the parts. In fact, you might consider hauling a wreck or two on the same trailer or truck whenever you haul home a good machine. This is called "liability averaging." If your spouse says something about you having money for yet another tractor but not enough for a new refrigerator, point indignantly to the tractors on the trailer—the beautiful one on steel and in running condition for which you paid $1,600 and the rusted hulks you got for $50 each. Then huff, "Snookums, I got those for a little more than $500 each and the one in the back is easily worth $2,000. That's a tidy profit of $400." See? Doesn't that make you sound like an investment wizard?

Rule 7: When things get critical, consider dragging home a tractor without a transmission or rear wheels. If there is complaint, you say, "Tractor? What tractor? That's not a tractor! That's only a front end. Not even close to a tractor." Then a couple weeks later bring home a rear end, minus the radiator, engine, and front wheels. "What tractor? That's no tractor! That's only a rear end. Not even close to a tractor." Don't try this, however, more than once every couple years.

Rule 8: Have a dealer or friend call you now and then when you're not at home and tell your spouse, "Rog told me to keep an eye on the Allis WC going at the auction Saturday, but it sold for $1,200 and I know there's no way a financially cautious and responsible guy like Rog would pay that much so I didn't even make a bid on it for him." Not only will this make you look real good, but the next time you do buy a tractor, say something like, "Lovie-bear, this beauty only cost me $300, which means we're $900 ahead of where we'd have been if I'd gotten the one before. If I keep saving money like this, we'll be able to go on a Caribbean cruise next winter." If you say it fast enough, it might work.

Rule 9: If your mate insults your work callin' it "rustoration" laugh a light-hearted laugh, making it clear that tractors are not to you what shoes are to Imelda Marcos.

Rule 10: If your situation worsens to the point where your mate asks, "Who do you love more, me or your tractors?" whatever you do, don't ask for time to think it over.

I've tried to couch this information in non-sexist language. Yes, I am dealing with my wife Linda—and what a darling she is! But there is every indication that my daughter Antonia is going to be a tractor nut like her Old Man and will use these same devices to smooth things over with her husband.

The above suggestions are not dishonest or deceptive, exactly. They are ways to make life easier for your spouse. In fact, now that I think about it, these acts of diplomacy are actually a kindness, a way to smooth the road for someone you love. Following Roger's Rules is a way of being a better person. People who follow Roger's Rules are *good* people.

Classic tractor

International Harvester's Farmall M made its debut in 1939, and has since become one of the all-time classic tractors. This restored M is owned by the Antique Gas & Steam Engine Museum in Vista, California. (Photograph by Vincent Manocchi)

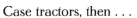

Case tractors, then . . .

ABOVE: *An early 1930s Case tractor runs a corn binder alongside a wagon pulled by a team. (Photograph by J. C. Allen and Son)*

. . . Case tractors, now

RIGHT: *A beautifully restored 1936 Case RC. Owner: John Bourque of St. Genevieve, Missouri. (Photograph by Ralph W. Sanders)*

UNEXPECTED ENTRANCE
By "JR" Gyger of Lebanon, Indiana

Times were tough when we were starting out, but I always managed to keep good equipment. I bought whatever land and latest Case equipment that came available in the neighborhood. I never liked to fix machinery, so keeping new equipment made life better and, I think, saved me money in the long run.

It was much later that I got into collecting and restoring old Case tractors for fun.

One incident still brings a smile to the face of my wife and me. Our youngest son, who was a bit on the wild side, came tearing into the garage on a DC Case we had added to the collection. The wife and I were sitting in the kitchen having a cup of coffee. Between the garage and the kitchen was a utility room with doors to the kitchen and to the garage. Well, the brakes on this DC were not what our son expected, and the next thing we knew, the door to the garage blasted open and the front wheels of the DC were in the utility room. Our oldest son still lives in the house, and evidence of the incident is still grooved into the threshold of that door.

Orchard tractors, then . . .

FACING PAGE: *With its protective fenders ensuring that tree limbs are not damaged by the wheels, a Case OC Orchard Special leads a spraying wagon while workers spray apples in the Goff Orchards near Sturgeon Bay, Wisconsin, in the 1930s. (Photograph by J. C. Allen and Son)*

. . . Orchard tractors, now

ABOVE: *A beautiful 1951 Oliver 77 Orchard model. Owner: Verlan Heberer of Belleville, Illinois. (Photograph by Ralph W. Sanders)*

RAMBLINGS AT THE THRESHERMEN'S REUNION
By Ed Klimuska of Lancaster County, Pennsylvania

Irvin Buchal lives on a dairy farm in Copenhagen, New York, with his wife Helen. He's retired, but keeps busy with his hobby: collecting old stuff. That includes tractors, tools, stone crushers, and gas engines.

"I collect anything old," Buchal says. "I have an old building full of stuff. I've collected a little bit of everything all my life." He calls the building a museum, and it's open to the public. "If I'm there, the door's unlocked," he adds. "If I'm not there, the doors are locked. We get people from all over. We even had people from Germany. People learn about the museum by word of mouth."

Is Mrs. Buchal involved with the museum?

"She gives me heck for collecting," Buchal says, with a laugh.

"No, I don't," Mrs. Buchal adds.

International, then and now
1954 Farmall 400 and 1995 Case-International 7220 Magnum. Owner: Don Rimathe of Huxley, Iowa. (Photograph by Ralph W. Sanders)

Vintage Oliver

The great Hart-Parr Company of Charles City, Iowa, was founded in 1897, and went on to offer a wide range of tractors, several of which were sold in Canada as early as the 1920s under Cockshutt's red-and-yellow colors, starting Cockshutt in the tractor business. Hart-Parr merged with Oliver in 1929, and subsequent tractors featured both firms' names for several years, as on this 1936 Oliver Hart-Parr 70 Row Crop. Owner: Jean L. Olson of Chatfield, Minnesota. (Photograph by Ralph W. Sanders)

Photography Index

A living history
The sun sets behind a vintage tractor, still at work. (Photograph by Jerry Irwin)